GARLAND STUDIES ON THE ELDERLY IN AMERICA

edited by

STUART BRUCHEY
University of Maine

A GARLAND SERIES

ELDERLY COHORT MIGRATION PATTERNS

METHODOLOGICAL PRESCRIPTIONS FOR FUTURE RESEARCH

JACK CARTER

GARLAND PUBLISHING, INC.
NEW YORK & LONDON / 1994

Library of Congress Cataloging-in-Publication Data

Carter, Jack, 1948–
    Elderly cohort migration patterns : methodological prescriptions
for future research / Jack Carter.
        p.   cm. — (Garland studies on the elderly in America)
    Includes bibliographical references and index.
    ISBN 0–8153–1652–6 (alk. paper)
    1. Aged—United States.   2. Migration, Internal—United States.
I. Title.   II. Series.
HQ1064.U5C36   1994
305.26'0973—dc20   93–48508
                                                              CIP

Printed on acid-free, 250-year-life paper
Manufactured in the United States of America

To the memory of my parents Jack and Margaret Banks Carter, my brother, Lawrence Carter, and my son, Chad Aaron Carter.

Contents

Preface

The initial stimulus that led to the writing of this book can be traced to work that I was doing at Florida State University's Center for the Study of Population in 1985-1986. At that time, I was assisting David Sly, then director of the center, in processing the 1940-1980 U.S. Census Bureau public use sample micro-data files. The 1940 and 1950 data were not widely available in computer readable form at that time, and we were some of the first investigators to work with them. This project involved not only getting the 1940 and 1950 data up and running, but constructing one huge data set containing all fifty years worth of data, with all of the variables recoded for comparability, where possible. This task took the better part of two years because there were more problems with processing and cleaning up the data than anyone had imagined, and, the faculty of the center and their assistants were working on a number of other projects simultaneously.

These data were subsequently used in a number of studies that all reflected one of the central reasons for the construction of the data set. That is, the desire to have the ability to do research that could examine not only age, but also period and cohort effects. Most of the studies in the sociology/economics of aging literature at that time were cross-sectional, and, although there had been numerous pieces published pointing out the need for multiple period and cohort research, data limitations were an ongoing barrier to accomplishing this. One of the limitations with our project, that we recognized from the start, was the limited number of variables relevant to any given study that were available in the micro files, and the even smaller number for which comparability was possible across all five censuses.

Because elderly migration is one of my areas of specialization, I had become very interested in the nature of the research literature that addressed this topic. I found that, almost since the beginning of interest in this area, there had been a proliferation of studies in elderly migration/local mobility that described the same sets of mover characteristics; those contained in the Census Bureau micro-data files. This gave me the initial idea for, and resulted in the first draft of, what was to become the present volume. The data set on which I had been working accorded an opportunity to do a study that included not only age, but also period and cohort effects. Furthermore, the same characteristics described in many cross-sectional studies could be examined from multiple period and cohort perspectives in an inferential framework to determine the extent of their predictive or explanatory power regarding elderly migratory behavior.

After completing the study that was to become this book, I condensed a portion of the material on elderly local mobility, and published it as a journal article (Carter, 1989). The literature update for that article convinced me that the issues detailed in the original study for elderly long-distance and local movers might well make a worthwhile addition to the literature. What I found in reviewing even more recent additions to the literature in these areas served to reinforce that conviction.

Elderly migration/mobility studies published since 1986 include some interesting additions to the literature. There are a number that represent variations on the above-mentioned descriptive "mover selectivity studies." For example, Yeats, Biggar, and Longino (1987) explore the effect that the distance of the move has on the characteristics of elderly interstate migrants. Cowper and Corcoran (1989) look at the same set of elderly long-distance mover characteristics, focusing on a comparison of elderly veterans and the general elderly population. Another expansion of the selectivity approach involves studies that describe both the same sets of mover characteristics and the characteristics of their areas of origin and destination (Serow, 1987; Serow and Charity, 1988; Voss et al., 1988; Serow, 1988; Spear and Meyer, 1988; Longino and Serow, 1992).

One of the most engaging developments in elderly migration research has been the relatively recent appearance of studies that are both theoretical and empirical. These studies represent a break from the general trend in the literature which contained mostly non-quantitative theoretical pieces, or atheoretical empirical studies. Several studies investigate and expand upon what has come to be called the Litwak-Longino Model, that posits a relationship between differing levels of instrumental disabilities and the propensity to move (Litwak and

Longino, 1987; Spear et al., 1991; Longino et al., 1991; Jackson et al., 1991; Bradisher et al., 1992).

Occasionally a study appears that examines the impact of cohort membership on elderly migration (e.g., Frey. 1986). However, there still seems to be a relative paucity of research that attempts to empirically disentangle the effects of age, period, and cohort. Thus this book project was born.

Within each section of the book, both elderly interstate migration and local (intracounty) mobility are addressed. The overall organization is like that used in many quantitative research reports, with the hypotheses developed and clearly stated, and the methods of analysis and results delineated and described. This format is certainly appropriate for a study of this scope, because the discussion section assimilates findings, and draws conclusions and implications relating to a number of issues.

The acknowledgements for this volume, with two exceptions, go back to my days at Florida State. The initiation and development of this project were made possible by suggestions from Dr. David F. Sly, for whom I worked from 1983-1986. Drs. William J. Serow, Michael Micklin, Charles B. Nam, Walter Terry and Isaac W. Eberstein, and Ms. Babs Rousseau all gave advice and assistance that was invaluable in completing the original study. I thank them for that and for their ongoing support. Mr. Jeremy Kerr, my research assistant at the University of New Orleans, was very helpful in aiding me with the library research that was necessary to update the original study, and Ms. Mary Dovie, of the Computer Resource Center at the University of New Orleans, has been absolutely selfless in producing the final copy for this book. Without their indispensable assistance, the present volume would not have been possible.

I. Introduction

This study examines elderly migration/mobility in the United States. Tables 2 and 3, and Figures 1-8, which are found in Chapter III, indicate definite differences in the patterns of cohort interstate migration and local mobility rates for the period 1940 through 1980. The research objective here is to point to more productive analytic strategies by attempting to explain these differences by putting into practice some of the methodological approaches that have been strongly precsribed for some time, but are rarely put into practice.

In this study the effects of age, period, and cohort on the volume of migration/mobility will be assessed. Characteristics of cohort components, i.e., the age groups making up each cohort at successive periods, will be expressed in terms of determinants of migration derived from the elderly migration/local mobility literature and those developed by the author. Hypotheses will be developed and tested which set forth the expected effects of cohort component characteristics on migration/mobility levels. Inter- and intracohort differences in these effects will also be considered.

The majority of elderly long- and short-distance residential mobility studies to date have been cross-sectional and focused on age differences, neglecting the effects of cohort or period. Although the importance of this earlier work is recognized and its contributions utilized in the present study, in which age and period effects are also examined, I hoped that this effort, by employing a cohort analysis, will go beyond those of the past. By identifying sets of factors that differentially affect elderly migration levels depending on cohort membership, we can begin to make more general theoretical statements regarding the kinds of social changes that underly these factors.

In recent years, and especially within the past decade, migration has been growing in importance relative to the other branches of demography as evidenced by the steady increase in migration research efforts. This is especially apparent with regard to the rising interest in internal migration within industrialized countries with low fertility and mortality, in which migration/mobility considerations constitute the most significant component of the dynamics of population change. Authors of local mobility studies are also noting with increasing frequency that the largest volume of population movement is occurring within counties (or comparable units) compared to the historically most often examined migration streams, e.g. those between states, regions, and the metropolitan and nonmetropolitan sectors. Furthermore, as the visibility of the elderly population has risen with increases in their absolute and proportionate numbers, there has been a proliferation of research on many aspects of aging, including elderly migration. Interest in elderly migration has been sustained in part by the assertions of authors such as Lee (1980) that this phenomenon has increased significantly since the 1940's and will continue to do so into the forseeable future. And there is a growing awareness by demographers of the need for work in the area of elderly local mobility, as this numerically largest segment of the elderly mobile population has been largely neglected by researchers.

Many authors have asserted the importance of a cohort perspective for understanding the dynamics of social change (e.g. Riley, 1985; Mason et al., 1973; Bengtson, 1985). Conceptual models in which society is conceived as an age stratification system within which individuals and successive cohorts of individuals are continually aging and important roles are age- graded have provided insights into the social process of aging from the perspectives of several disciplines (e.g. Lazarsfeld, [1944] 1960; Neugarten, 1966; Brim, 1966; Clausen, 1968; Baltes et al., 1980; Abeles, 1981). This general approach has brought together two central theoretical perspectives on aging, one focusing on the consequences of variations in age structure (Sorokin, 1941,1947; Parsons, 1942; Linton, 1942; Eisenstadt, 1956), and the other emphasizing the importance of unique cohort characteristics that result from experiencing particular historical events for the dynamics of social change (Mannheim, [1928] 1952); Cain, 1964; Ryder, 1965).

Ryder (1964) sets forth an important principle about the dynamic interplay between individual aging and social change. That is, because of social change, different cohorts cannot grow up and grow old in precisely the same way. This observation has led to increasing interest in cohort analysis as a means to understanding behavior related to changes in the age- stratified social structure and the aging patterns of successive cohorts. Various authors studying diverse research problems have posited the necessity of distinguishing the effects of cohort membership from the effects of particular periods (e.g. Oppenheim, 1970; Ryder, 1965; Keyfitz, 1972; Winsborough, 1972). Thus it has been established through studies in which age, period, and cohort have conceptually distinct causal impacts on the dependent variable that the resolution of a number of substantive research issues requires the consideration of all three perspectives in a cohort analysis.

Many recent research efforts have demonstrated the importance of the interplay of cohort differences and social change. In a study of the effect of the continually increasing levels of educational attainment by women in the past two centuries, Uhlenberg (1979) points out the enormous effects on behavior related to marriage and having children, labor force participation, and ranges of interests and friendships, etc. He asserts that as more women in each successive cohort achieve increasingly high levels of education and lead their lives in new ways, social norms and institutions are altered, demonstrating that social changes have affected the lives of women in successive cohorts, who in turn have contributed to the restructuring of the institutions in which they participate.

Other authors have cited the phenomenon of "cohort norm formation", which results from the common historical era and events shared by each cohort's members (e.g. Elder, 1979; Riley, 1978; Mannheim, [1928] 1952). As a result of the common patterns of response developed by cohort members, "...each cohort exerts a collective force as it moves through the age-stratified society, pressing for adjustments in social roles and social values (Riley, 1985:403)". Glenn (1980) suggests that this process is still operative for cohort members at the oldest ages.

One way to demonstrate the importance of utilizing a cohort oriented research perspective is to point out the types of fallacies of interpretation that can and have resulted from the "deceptive simplicity" of cross-sectional data (Riley, 1973). Cross-sectional differences in an independent variable involve people who are in different life stages (approximated by age), as well as being from different cohorts. Riley (1973) points out that since period differences reflect a combination of life-course differences and cohort differences, the researcher is in danger of committing the "life- course fallacy", i.e., overlooking the cohort effect, which can be as bad or worse than the converse "generational fallacy", which results from not considering the possibility of life- course differences. She further points out the importance, when using longitudinal data, of avoiding the fallacy of "cohort-centrism", i.e. generalizing about aging and social change from the viewpoint of a single cohort. This can be accomplished through a true "cohort analysis" involving comparisons of the life-course patterns of successive cohorts, and the effects of historical/environmental correlates (Riley, 1973:37-42).

Hobcraft et al. (1982) have also pointed out the importance of a cohort perspective for demographers in particular. They assert that the most important question regarding age- period-cohort anaylsis in demographic research involves the substantive importance of cohort influences. That is, do the age patterns of individuals who were born in the same year or period respond to cohort influences as well as to period influences, making it impossible to describe the experience of a cohort completely in terms of age and period effects? Or, are the experiences of a cohort largely determined by age-specific period effects that coincide with ages of greater or lesser susceptibility? They further argue that demographers have a pragmatic as well as a theoretical interest in these issues because : "In the past, period-based calculations led demographers to conclusions and predictions that later experience proved wrong. As a result, the relationship of a period- specific measure to the remaining life experience of cohorts active in that period has become as compelling a question for demographers as is the delineation of age, period, and cohort effects" (Hobcraft et al.,1982:5).

The utilization of a cohort perspective is especially important for studies of elderly migration/mobility. Even though the age effect on these phenomena is certainly important, the older ages having been recognized as a life stage milestone at which an upsurge in levels of migration/mobility might well be expected to occur, the special significance of the interplay of cohort differences and social change for the elderly has been posited in the literature. Torrey (1982) provides an example of cohort- social change feedback processes in an examination of men's retirement practices over time. She points to changes such as those in the character of occupations and the expansion of pension plans, which have resulted in increasingly earlier ages of retirement throughout the twentieth century. These cohort differences, in addition to increases in longevity, have resulted in many added retirement years and marked changes in the income, social involvement, leisure activities, health and effective functioning of the elderly, which in turn have affected many social norms and institutions. These and other studies (e.g. Michael et al., 1980) that point out the effect of social changes in parental authority, birth rates, longevity, etc. on kinship relations, including the marital status of the elderly, demonstrate the importance of understanding the feedback loops that characterize the relationship between cohort flow and changing age structure.

In the following chapter, studies relevant to this research are discussed. Three basic types of work are included in this literature review. The first are the more conventional investigations of elderly migration/mobility. Then the studies examining elderly migration from a cohort perspective, and those positing the need for such studies are cited and sumarized. The final section of Chapter II is a discussion of the ways in which the broader scope of the present study may make it possible to go beyond the findings of much of the existing literature in this area.

II. Literature Review

ELDERLY MIGRATION/MOBILITY

The elderly migration/mobility literature that is not specifically concerned with a cohort perspective nonetheless contains articles that are concerned with the effects of age and other migrant characteristics on elderly migration. The findings of these studies can be very useful in pointing to effective approaches for examining cohort migration patterns. Age, as used in social research, is really a proxy for biological and environmental determinants that are highly correlated with chronological age, e.g. entering into and exiting from age-graded roles and role clusters (Baltes and Willis, 1979; Riley et al., 1972). Therefore, the assumption and relinquishment of various roles clustered within various age ranges of the life course has been at least implicit in studies that point to the relation of age and migration (e.g. Lee, 1966; Starr, 1972).

Many studies have associated the acceleration of migration from the teens to a peak in the twenties with the transition to adulthood and its attendant role changes, i.e., completing one's education, going to work and possibly changing jobs for a time, getting married and starting a family, and so on (e.g. Lee, 1966, 1980; Hogan, 1981; Winsborough, 1978, 1979). The downturn in migration following the twenties has been attributed to the increased family- and career-oriented ties and bonds that are part of the "settling in" process (e.g. Speare, 1974).

Of special interest for this study, of course, is research that points to age-related migration patterns within the older ages. An upswing in migration during the "young elderly" ages has often been attributed to moves associated with retirement (e.g. Chevan and Fischer, 1979: Lee, 1980; Wiseman, 1980; Heaton et al., 1980). Lee's (1980) article sets forth this orientation as it has been used by most other authors. He asserts that there is an upswing in elderly migration with retirement for different reasons, depending on the characteristics of the migrants. The motivation is in part due to a need to adapt to new housing needs and cut living costs. He further asserts that for both the less and more affluent elderly, migration is most often to areas where the elderly can enjoy leisure pursuits with other elderly persons.

The other side of the coin with regard to age-related migration patterns among the elderly that is depicted in the literature is seen in the assertions that migration increases among the older elderly are attributable to life changes such as declining health, loss of a spouse, and increasing economic/social dependence, (Wiseman, 1980; Patrick, 1980; Longino, 1980; Yee and van Arsdol, 1977; Longino, 1979). Longino (1980) examines this orientation with regard to metropolitan and nonmetropolitan elderly migration. He argues that there appears to be selection among nonmetropolitan to metropolitan elderly movers for the older and more economically and socially dependent elderly, and suggests the possibility that the more fully developed age-related services in metropolitan areas are pulling elderly migrants in need of various types of assistance. In a 1979 article the same author found that elderly migrants returning to the state of their birth after having experienced post-retirement migration, were negatively selected for socioeconomic characteristics relative to other elderly interstate migrants, i.e., they tended to be the more dependent elderly. He again asserts that these results are consistent with a model of moves among the older, more dependent elderly when service and social support needs increase; in this case, secondary post-retirement moves to state of birth.

More typical of the studies positing an elderly assistance/mobility hypothesis are those that examine differences in the characteristics of elderly long distance migrants and elderly local movers. Local elderly residential mobility is examined from a social characteristics perspective by Biggar (1980) who compares the demographic, socioeconomic, and housing characteristics of elderly local movers and migrants from 1965-1970. She found that elderly migrants tend to be, for example, from the higher educational and income strata and to be married with a spouse present, and that this "positive selectivity" increases with the distance of the move. However, the pattern of selectivity for elderly local movers is the opposite, with selection being from the more economically/socially dependent strata. She also found that both interstate and local movers tend to be both white and female. These conclusions regarding elderly local mobility are supported to some extent by studies finding that the reasons for local mobility most frequently cited by the elderly are declining health and the need for assistance (Goldscheider, 1966; Lenzer, 1965; Lawton et al., 1973; Pastalan, 1975; Ables, 1981).

A study by Rives and Serow (1981) examines the relationships of age and other migrant characteristics to elderly migration in more detail. They find a steady decrease in interstate migration flows for five-year age groups from 55-64 through 85+. They also conclude that elderly migration streams are dominated by female movers, and that the concentration of females increases generally with age.

Descriptive studies that focus on the places of origin and places of destination of elderly migrants are well represented in the literature. A 1980 study by Cynthia Flynn compares states of origin and destination for general and elderly interstate migrants. She finds that there is much less difference in the most frequent states of origin for the two populations than for the states of destination, the top ten elderly destination states accounting for a higher proportion of overall migration than with the general migrant population. Florida and California are shown to account for a third of all elderly interstate in-migration, as opposed to 18 percent of in-migration of the general population.

In the same vein, two articles by Biggar (1980a), and Biggar et al. (1980) examine elderly migration streams in terms of states of origin and states of destination. The former article points out that over half of elderly migrants moved to fifteen Sunbelt states, and the latter examines states representative of the seven major regional areas of elderly in- and out-migration. Both articles discuss the economic effects of elderly migration flows on sending and receiving states. These discussions are based on the reestablishment of the above- mentioned assertions regarding the positive selection of elderly interstate migrants for social and socioeconomic characteristics in relation to those who do not move or move locally, and similar assertions regarding the differential selection of elderly migrants to various regional destinations.

There are a few examples to be found in the elderly migration literature of studies that are longitudinal, at least to some degree. It is not surprising that studies concerned with the metropolitan/nonmetropolitan migration "turnaround" would involve a longitudinal analysis, because it is necessary to examine migration at more than one date in order to identify a point of reversal of migration patterns. One study (Fuguitt and Tordella, 1980) focusing on the elderly contribution to the nonmetropolitan migration "turnaround", utilizes 1950, '60, and '70 Census data, and 1975 estimates prepared by the Census Bureau. They find that population redistribution due to total migration favored metropolitan areas until 1970, and that elderly migrants were pioneers of the nonmetropolitan turnaround, in that elderly nonmetropolitan migration rates are positive and exceed metropolitan rates in the 1960's as well as in the 1970's.

In a 1980 article Heaton et al. focus on migration between metropolitan and nonmetropolitan areas by males 45 years and over who are in and out of the labor force   for 1955-60, 1965-70, and 1970-75. The results indicate that males are more likely to move to nonmetropolitan areas from metropolitan areas if they are retired, and suggest the increasing importance of quality-of-life considerations in migration decisions.

Rives and Serow (1978) analyze 1960 and 1970 Census data in a study of elderly return migration for 1955-60 and 1965-70. Changes in the volume and rate of elderly and nonelderly return migration for these two periods are reported.   The findings indicate that persons of retirement age are less likely to migrate than the general population, with regard to all interstate migration as well as return migration. However, the results also point out that during the ten-year interval the rate of return migration increased at a greater rate for the elderly than for the general population, and that return migration is more frequent in the elderly than in the general migration stream.

Biggar et al. (1984), in a study of selectivity and trends in elderly migration patterns in which social characteristics e.g. sex, race, marital status, education, and income were considered, found that selectivity patterns for the 1955-1960 and the 1965-1970 periods varied little, with the elderly from the more independent households and socioeconomic ranks migrating more. The specific findings indicate that, in terms of migrant characteristics, the trends for the decade examined include: slightly lower proportions of women, whites, and widows, and somewhat higher mean levels of education for interstate migrants; and slightly higher proportions of women, whites, and widows, and somewhat higher mean levels of education for local movers.

THE COHORT PERSPECTIVE-ELDERLY
MIGRATION/MOBILITY

For over forty years, investigators have pointed to the need for studies of migration/mobility utilizing a cohort approach. In her Research Memorandum on Migration Differentials Dorothy Swaine Thomas (1938:416- 417) asserts that the best method of classifying persons according to migrant status "...is one which preserves the time sequence of migratory acts during the life span or during part of the life span of the individuals studied". However, practically none of the hundreds of studies cited in the "Memorandum" apply such a method. In the years since then, the need for longitudinal or cohort studies of migration has been expressed by many others (e.g. Folger, 1958; Duncan, 1958).

In a 1980 article outlining the most pressing needs regarding future directions in elderly migration research, Stephen Golant (1980) lists the separation of cohort, age, and period effects as one of six priority topics for future research in the area of aging and migration. However, in spite of the increasingly wide-spread recognition of the importance of both cohort analyses and migration studies, the examination of demographic processes utilizing a cohort perspective has almost exclusively been limited to topics relating to fertility or mortality. This fact has been pointed out by authors surveying the use of the cohort framework in demographic studies since its usefulness was demonstrated over two decades ago by authors like Hastings and Berry (1979) and Hobcraft et al. (1982). Therefore, the literature in this area must be described in terms of the few notable exceptions to the above observations.

One such exception is a study by Hope T. Eldridge (1964) which applies a cohort approach to the analysis of migration differentials. This ground-breaking research examines the age- specific cohort migration rates of native white males in the United States from 1870-1880 to 1940-1950 with regard to the relative levels of economic activity for each decade, i.e., whether the decade was "prosperous" or "depressed". Her findings indicate that while there are definite age effects on migration patterns corresponding to major life-stage factors, these effects are mitigated by whether or not a given cohort reached peak migration ages at the end of a prosperous or a depressed decade.

"...[T]he rates of all cohorts either fluctuate in concert with alternating levels of economic activity or show a modified response in the form of slowing or accelerating rates of fall" (Eldridge,1964: 217). Of particular interest for the present study is her assertion that the preceding finding "...does not bear out Thomas' speculation that migration at ages above 55 may be 'noneconomic,'i.e., go counter to economic levels (Eldridge, 1964:217)".

Karl E. Taeuber (1966) renews the call for cohort migration studies. He points out the deficiencies of studies using the "migration expectancy" approach, which involves a life- table-like synthetic cohort approach, and those using a true cohort approach to examine net migration rates. One of his main theses is that the problems found in the latter can be overcome through the use of complete residence histories.

In a cohort analysis of black and white migration patterns, Pitcher et al. (1985) state that since the Eldridge (1964) and Taeuber (1966) studies little attention has been given to cohort analyses of migration. The main issues addressed by Pitcher et al. are how age, period, and cohort simultaneously affect migration rates, and how these effects vary by race.

THE ELDERLY MIGRATION/MOBILITY LITERATURE AND THE PRESENT STUDY

In a 1980 review of the state of elderly migration studies in the United States, Gladys Bowles asserts, like the authors cited in the previous section, that a major deficiency of much of the work in the area of elderly migration to date is the lack of an appropriate theoretical orientation. She further points out the counter productive nature of the most common responses by researchers to this situation: either being unconcerned by this deficiency or decrying the fact that they do not find theories suitable to their endeavors. In conclusion, she states that "...[p]erhaps one of the greatest challenges of research on migration of the elderly is the design of studies that can contribute to theory development while at the same time providing research results that are timely, interesting, and useful" (Bowles, 1980: Pp. 140).

The vast majority of the studies in the elderly migration literature are cross-sectional and atheoretical. Although most of the studies cited above have been important exploratory efforts in a relatively new area of investigation, for the most part, they look at age effects and make generalizations without any real consideration of cohort or even period effects. The point has surely been reached at which limited usefulness will result from the further repetition and replication of such studies. My hope is that in this book will help clarify these issues by putting into practice some of the above suggestions for improving the situation regarding the state of elderly migration theory development. I see no problem with utilizing "partial theories" e.g. life cycle orientated perspectives, especially during the formative stages of an area of investigation. However, it is asserted here that life cycle and social characteristics orientations as they have been employed thus far may not yet have legitimately achieved the status of partial theories. An argument could be made that at their present stage of development they are in fact methodologies and not theories at all.

The kinds of descriptive cross-sectional studies that have been done to date have largely viewed the migrant population as the universe, and examined the percent of the population that possess certain demographic, social and socioeconomic characteristics. There is nothing wrong with establishing empirical regularities in the quest to develop models for understanding social/demographic phenomena. However, the repeated examination of cross-sectional data for a single period is not sufficient to accomplish this goal. (Most of the literature cited above utilizes 1960, 1970, or 1980 U.S. Census data.) This approach does not demonstrate whether or not the characteristics so often examined are useful in the development of models for explaining or predicting elderly migration/ mobility behavior.

The present study uses recently available data in order to apply a somewhat more sophisticated methodological approach to the examination of elderly migration/mobility using many of the variables repeatedly found in the studies to date. The availability of five decades of U.S. Census Public Use Sample Microdata for 1940-1980 makes it possible to undertake types of analyses never before done. The present study will involve a cohort analysis, and an examination of period as well as age effects, regarding the relationships of some of the characteristics most often found in elderly migration/mobility studies. It is hoped that this multi-dimensional approach will shed some light on the validity of some of the generalizations made from observed relationships in traditional studies, involving the tabulation of variables thought to be related to elderly migration, and the extent to which these studies are pointing in useful directions for the development of a more integrated theoretical framework. This approach should suggest ways in which future studies can contribute to the accumulation of research findings that will increase the empirical basis for a theoretical framework to guide the study of elderly migration/mobility.

III. Data and Methodology

DATA DESCRIPTION

The data to be utilized in this study are from the 1940, 1950, 1960, 1970, and 1980 United States Bureau of the Census Public Use Sample micro-data files. These data permit the production of detailed tabulations for variables contained in the long forms of each census, constrained only by sample size. Analysis across censuses is also possible since the consistency of definitions and coding across the censuses can be assessed and the appropriate adjustments made, where possible. These data are particularly well-suited for cohort analysis because they allow the researcher the flexibility to use census-derived data in the same manner as data collected from a survey.

In spite of the unique characteristics resulting from the above-mentioned constraints or the situations under which they were developed, each of the census micro files was constructed in the same general manner from samples drawn by the same general parameters. That is, each of these files represents a stratified (one percent) sample of the population in the Census year drawn from those households that received the long-form questionnaire. Persons not in households (those in institutions and other group quarters) who received the long form questionnaires were sampled on an individual basis.

Sample size is not problematic, as demonstrated in Table 1 which provides the populations for five-year age groups 50-89 and 90 and over. Although sample sizes are smallest at the oldest ages in the earliest censuses, even the 1940 and 1950 public use samples yield more than 3,800 and 5,800 persons 85 and over, respectively.

Table 1: AGE DISTRIBUTIONS FOR THE OLDER U.S. POPULATION:
1940-1980 FOR FIVE YEAR AGE GROUPS, 50-90>

AGE	1940	1950	1960	1970	1980
50-54	7188400	8385960	10025000	11172000	11662000
55-59	5737100	7273860	8606100	9968400	11686160
60-64	4626800	6104010	7156600	8600400	10218960
65-69	3798300	5012370	6151600	7025700	8888160
70-74	2522900	3447510	4650100	5469700	6887120
75-79	1452800	2179650	2961500	3886300	4835780
80-84	772700	1171500	1482500	2299900	2966560
85-89	280300	439560	640200	1027900	1510080
90>	105500	143220	212500	500600	705800

Source: U.S. Bureau of the Census

Differing concepts and definitions used in each Census, and the addition and deletion of items from one Census to the next are another constraint which the data place on the analyses. Age, a key variable in this study, is illustrative of one type of problem resulting from basic coding practices for variables which are conceptually the same from one Census to the next, but for which coding changed in the production of the micro files. For 1940-1970 age is reported in single years through 99, with a final category of 100 and over, while for 1980 age is coded in single years through 89, with a final category of 90 and over. This means, of course, that the earlier years must be recoded so that the oldest age category for all years will be 90 and over. This constraint is not problematic for the present research, especially given the known unreliability of age reporting at the oldest ages. Problems involving changes in concepts, such as the difference in the 1940- 1970 "head of household", and the 1980 "householder" will not pose major difficulties for the present analysis because they do not directly affect the variables used.

The most significant comparability problem for the present study involves the dependent variable, "migration status". In 1950, the question regarding place of residence in the past, which is the basis for establishing mobility status, referred to residence one year earlier rather than five years earlier as in all of the other 1940-1980 Censuses. Thus the residential mobility data for 1950 are based on a one year interval, 1949-1950, rather than a five-year interval. Thus the age-specific migration rates for 1950 must be adjusted in order to make them comparable to similar rates for the other census years.

Justification for these adjustments is found in Census Bureau assertions regarding the consistency of response in the mobility question. They point out the close correspondence of the 1950 census data and the Current Population Survey (CPS) data for roughly the same period (U.S. Bureau of the Census, 1957). The percentage distributions for previous residence categories from the two sources are as follows:

Residence in 1949	CPS	1950 Census
Same House	80.9	82.6
Different House,		
Same County	13.1	11.4
Different County,		
Same State	3.0	3.0
Different State	2.6	2.6
Abroad	.3	.4

Since similar CPS one-year mobility data are available from 1947-1948 forward, the proportions derived by dividing the number of interstate and local movers found in the 1949- 1950 CPS data by the total numbers of such movers for the five-year period 1947-1948 to 1951-1952 from CPS data for each of these years can be applied to the 1950 Census interstate and intracounty mover distributions in order to make them comparable to the five-year data from the other Censuses. These proportions are as follows:

Age	Interstate Migration	Local Mobility
45-64	.1879	.1887
65>	.1552	.1998

The inverse of these proportions are used as the adjustment factors to be applied to the 1950 1- year migration/mobility rates (e.g. 1/.1897 = 5.32, in the case of interstate migration for those 45-64). Therefore, non-elderly interstate migration rates and local mobility rates are adjusted by factors of 5.32 and 5.30, respectively, and elderly interstate migration rates and local mobility rates are adjusted by factors of 6.44 and 5.01, respectively. These adjustments are generally consistent with the Census Bureau's assertion that mobility levels for the 1949-1950 period are probably somewhat lower than for the rest of the post-World War II years because this period involved a slight economic recession, relative to surrounding years.

Tables 2 and 3 contain the rates of interstate migration and rates of local mobility for the 50-years-and-over U.S. population, 1940 through 1980, per 100 population. The 1950 rates are adjusted as described above. These are five-year migration rates presented for five-year age groups, with the estimated age- specific beginning-of-migration/mobility period, or mid-decade, population used as the denominator. The data

Table 2: **RATES OF U.S. INTERSTATE MIGRATION, 1940–1980 PER 100 POPULATION**

Birth Period	50-54	55-59	60-64	65-69	70-74	75-79	80-84	85-89	90>	
1925-1929	5.02									
1920-1924		5.00								
1915-1919	4.32		5.52							
1910-1914		3.86		5.90						
1905-1909	5.25		4.12		4.64					
1900-1904		4.54		4.62		4.22				
1895-1899	7.87		4.36		4.05		4.36			
1890-1894		6.86		4.87		3.43		5.24		
1885-1889	3.61		6.44		4.51		3.83		5.38	1980
1880-1884		3.70		7.79		3.96		4.40		
1875-1879			3.48		8.24		4.03		5.14	1970
1970-1874				2.91		8.76		3.95		
1865-1869					2.81		8.11		4.55	1960
1860-1864						2.88		4.70		
1855-1859							2.81		3.41	1950
1850-1854								3.01		
Pre-1850									5.23	1940

Source: U.S. Bureau of the Census

Table 3: **RATES OF U.S. LOCAL MOBILITY, 1940–1980 PER 100 POPULATION**

Birth Period	50-54	55-59	60-64	65-69	70-74	75-79	80-84	85-89	90>	
1925-1929	16.44									
1920-1924		15.20								
1915-1919	17.92		14.06							
1910-1914		17.51		14.14						
1905-1909	27.39		16.55		14.06					
1900-1904		24.08		15.83		14.84				
1895-1899	42.45		22.46		15.80		17.22			
1890-1894		39.86		21.43		16.75		21.62		
1885-1889	42.90		36.94		21.94		19.99		24.22	1980
1880-1884		40.85		35.22		22.04		22.48		
1875-1879			39.37		35.12		22.65		25.38	1970
1970-1874				40.44		34.42		25.49		
1865-1869					38.05		36.22		29.29	1960
1860-1864						36.26		39.03		
1855-1859							36.78		37.22	1950
1850-1854								37.30		
Pre-1850									32.76	1940

Source: U.S. Bureau of the Census

in these two tables are arranged so that age-specific period rates for each of the five years can be read diagonally and rates for the same age group across the five periods can be read vertically. Age-specific rates for period-of-birth cohorts can be found reading horizontally, with the periods of birth, "before 1850" to "1925 to 1929" designated at the far left. These cohort migration rates are of particular interest in the present study. Distinct differences in the patterns of migration/mobility rates for different cohorts, and in the patterns of interstate versus local mobility rates for the same cohort can be seen in Figures 1-8.

HYPOTHESES

The literature cited above suggests expected relationships of certain characteristics, e.g. being female (Rives and Serow, 1981; Biggar, 1980), being white (Steiner et al., 1985; Biggar, 1980; Biggar, 1984), having a spouse present (Biggar, 1980a; Biggar et al., 1980), and level of educational attainment (Longino, 1979; Biggar et al, 1984) with levels of migration and levels of local mobility. Regarding interstate migration, it has been asserted that migrants tend to be female and white, and that they are positively selected in terms of social characteristics e.g. education and marital status (i.e., they tend to be married with a spouse present). The main hypotheses that follow reflect these assertions.   The subhypothesis that accompanies each main hypothesis addresses the expected effect of period-of-birth cohort membership on the relationship set forth in the main hypothesis.

H1. The percent of the population that is female is positively related to rates of interstate migration.

Although the proportion of the older population that is female has increased, the older female population has increasingly assumed characteristics that are thought to be nonconducive to interstate migration, in terms of marital and relative socioeconomic status. Therefore, it is hypothesized that:

H1a. Membership in more recent birth cohorts will weaken the positive relationship hypothesized in H1.

Figure   1:   PATTERNS OF COHORT INTERSTATE MIGRATION
                   RATES PER 100 POPULATION

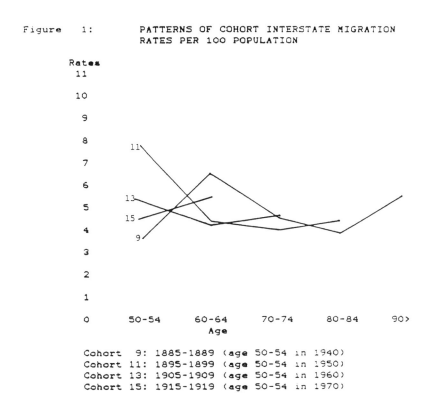

Cohort 9: 1885-1889 (age 50-54 in 1940)
Cohort 11: 1895-1899 (age 50-54 in 1950)
Cohort 13: 1905-1909 (age 50-54 in 1960)
Cohort 15: 1915-1919 (age 50-54 in 1970)

Source: U.S. Bureau of the Census

Figure 2:   PATTERNS OF COHORT INTERSTATE MIGRATION
                 RATES PER 100 POPULATION

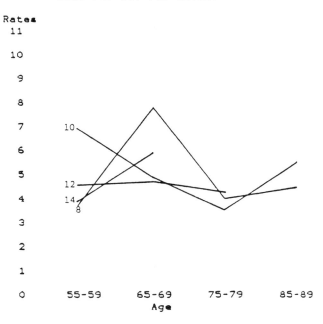

Cohort 8: 1880-1884 (age 55-59 in 1940)
Cohort 10: 1890-1894 (age 55-59 in 1950)
Cohort 12: 1900-1904 (age 55-59 in 1960)
Cohort 14: 1910-1914 (age 55-59 in 1970)

Source: U.S. Bureau of the Census

Figure 3:   PATTERNS OF COHORT LOCAL MOBILITY
              RATES PER 100 PERSONS

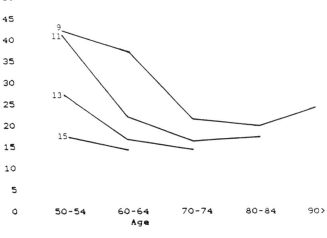

        Cohort 9: 1885-1889 (age 50-54 in 1940)
        Cohort 11: 1895-1899 (age 50-54 in 1950)
        Cohort 13: 1905-1909 (age 50-54 in 1960)
        Cohort 15: 1915-1919 (age 50-54 in 1970)

Source: U.S. Bureau of the Census

Figure 4:   PATTERNS OF COHORT LOCAL MOBILITY RATES
                 PER 100 POPULATION

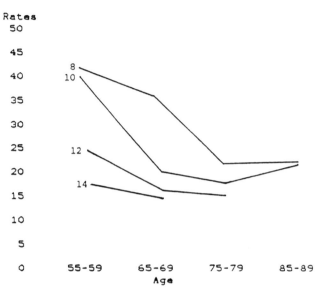

Cohort 8: 1880-1884 (age 55-59 in 1940)
Cohort 10: 1890-1894 (age 55-59 in 1950)
Cohort 12: 1900-1904 (age 55-59 in 1960)
Cohort 14: 1910-1914 (age 55-59 in 1970)

Source: U.S. Bureau of the Census

Figure 5:   COHORT 9 PATTERNS OF INTERSTATE AND LOCAL
Rates   MIGRATION RATES PER 100 POPULATION

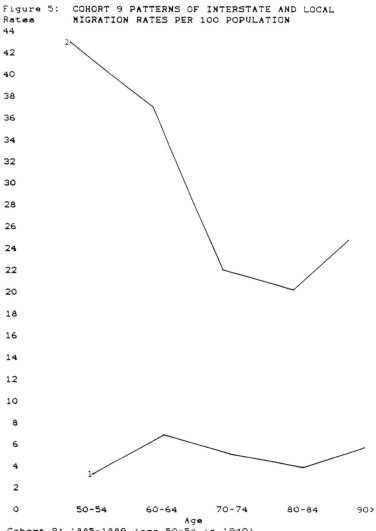

Cohort 9: 1885-1889 (age 50-54 in 1940)
Interstate Migration - 1.
Local Mobility ------- 2. Source: U.S. Bureau of the Census

Figure 6: PATTERNS OF COHORT 11 INTERSTATE AND LOCAL
Rates   RATES PER 100 PERSONS

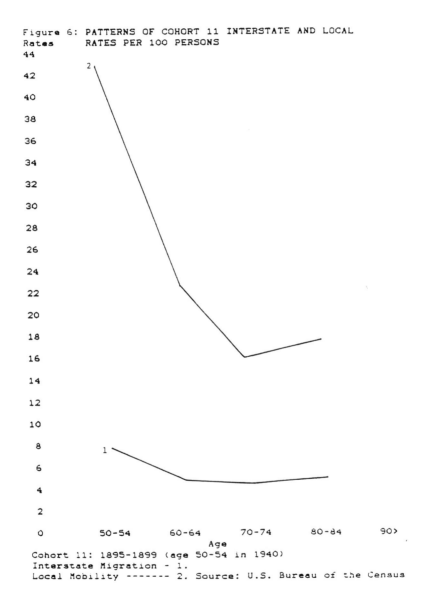

Cohort 11: 1895-1899 (age 50-54 in 1940)
Interstate Migration - 1.
Local Mobility ------- 2. Source: U.S. Bureau of the Census

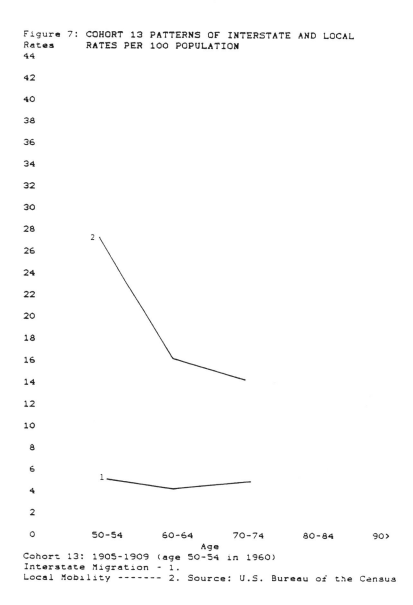

Figure 7: COHORT 13 PATTERNS OF INTERSTATE AND LOCAL
Rates   RATES PER 100 POPULATION

Cohort 13: 1905-1909 (age 50-54 in 1960)
Interstate Migration - 1.
Local Mobility ------- 2. Source: U.S. Bureau of the Census

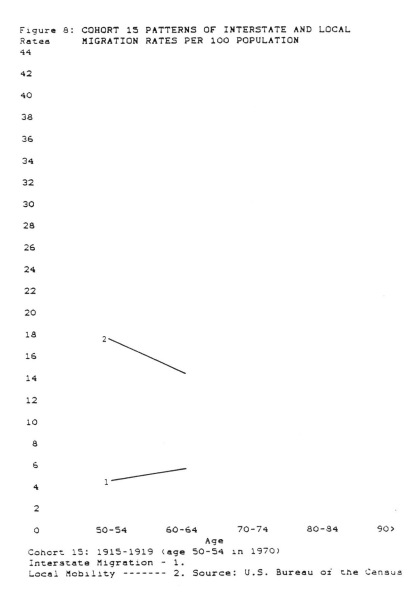

Figure 8: COHORT 15 PATTERNS OF INTERSTATE AND LOCAL
Rates   MIGRATION RATES PER 100 POPULATION

Cohort 15: 1915-1919 (age 50-54 in 1970)
Interstate Migration - 1.
Local Mobility ------- 2. Source: U.S. Bureau of the Census

H2. The percent of the population that is white is positively related to rates of interstate migration.

Since the literature suggests slight increases in non-white migration levels (Biggar et al., 1984), and non-whites are becoming more socioeconomically heterogeneous, it is hypothesized that:

H2a. Membership in more recent birth cohorts will weaken the relationship set forth in H2.

H3. The percent of the population without a spouse is negatively related to rates of interstate migration.

It is asserted in the literature (Biggar et al., 1984) that recent decade trends indicate an increase in the positive selection of interstate elderly migrants, in terms of marital and socioeconomic status. Therefore, it is hypothesized that:

H3a. Membership in more recent birth cohorts will strengthen the relationship set forth in H3.

H4. Mean years of completed education is positively related to rates of interstate migration.

According to the rationale associated with H3a, the following should be true:

H4a. Membership in more recent birth cohorts will strengthen the relationship set forth in H4.

The magnitude of completed fertility should have direct implications for the discretionary income and time of older persons. Having fewer children, which these data show to have most often been accompanied by an earlier schedule of completed fertility, should mean that children are out of the home earlier, allowing more freedom and resources for their parents to engage in long distance migration. It is therefore hypothesized that:

H5. The mean number of children ever born is negatively related to rates of interstate migration.

Since schedules of completed fertility have tended to become earlier historically (U.S. Department of Health, Education, and Welfare, 1976), the effect of fewer children should increase. Therefore, it is hypothesized that:

H5a. Membership in more recent birth cohorts will strengthen the relationship set forth in H5.

The literature indicates that local movers, like longer distance migrants, tend to be female and white. However, all evidence points to negative selection of local movers in terms of social and socioeconomic characteristics e.g. education and marital status. As with the preceding hypotheses, subhypotheses are presented addressing the effect of membership in more recent birth cohorts on the relationships set forth in each main hypothesis.

H6. The percent of the population that is female is positively related to rates of local mobility.

Changes in male/female differential longevity and changes in living arrangements resulting in more older people living apart from younger family members would indicate that:

H6a. Membership in more recent birth cohorts should strengthen the relationship set forth in H6.

H7. The percent of the population that is white is positively related to rates of local mobility.

Since the literature (Biggar et al., 1984) indicates recent slight increases in non-white mobility, it should follow that:

H7a. Membership in more recent birth cohorts will weaken the relationship set forth in H7.

H8. The percent of the population without a spouse is positively related to rates of local mobility.

By the same reasoning associated with H6a it should follow that:

H8a. Membership in more recent birth cohorts will strengthen the relationship set forth in H8.

H9. Mean years of completed education is negatively related to rates of local mobility.

The literature indicates (Biggar et al., 1984) that recent decade trends show an increase in the mean level of education for local movers. Therefore, it is hypothesized that:

H9a. Membership in more recent birth cohorts will weaken the relationship set forth in H9.

The literature suggests (e.g. Wiseman, 1980; Biggar, 1980; Goldscheider, 1966) that many local moves among the older population are assistance related. Since only a small percentage of the elderly are institutionalized, having more children might well increase the chances that an older person would have someplace to go when the need arises. Therefore it is hypothesized that:

H10. The mean number of children ever born is positively related to rates of local mobility.

The changes in living arrangements referred to above would indicate that elderly parents are increasingly living separately from their children during the time frame of this study . Therefore, it is hypothesized that:

H10a. Membership in more recent birth cohorts will strengthen the relationship set forth in H10.

VARIABLE DESCRIPTION

As indicated above, the independent variables utilized in this study are demographic and socioeconomic characteristics and period conditions derived from the literature cited or introduced specifically for this study. The dependent variable is levels of migration/mobility, which is measured using the "migration status", or "recent migration" variable found in the 1940-1980 micro files. This variable is actually based on what is commonly referred to as the "five-year question", which asks respondents where they lived five years previous to the census date. Through recoding, it is possible to obtain five comparable categories for the five censuses indicating that five years previous to the census the respondent lived: (1) in the same house, (2) in a different house, same county (3) in a different county, same state, (4) in a different state, or (5) abroad. Thus, nonmovers and intracounty (local), intrastate, interstate, and international movers can be identified. The present study is focused on interstate migration and local mobility. These data are used as the numerators for constructing rates of migration, such as those presented in Tables 1 and 2 (with estimated beginning of migration/mobility period populations as denominators), and in the regression analyses to follow. The possible distortions resulting from measuring migration/mobility levels using a residence-at-a-previous-time question have been extensively discussed (e.g. Shryock, 1964; U.S. Census Bureau, 1963; Canada, Dominion Bureau of Statistics, 1965; Japan, Bureau of Statistics, 1962) and will not be reiterated here. However, many researchers have concluded that in the absence of data from a continuous population register or some other source of complete residence histories, migration/mobility data such as those obtainable from the Census micro data files can be effectively utilized, and valuable insights into migration behavior have resulted.

Age. Obviously, in any study concerned with age, cohort, and period effects on migration/mobility as well as cohort and period, age-specific characteristics and levels of migration, age is a very important independent variable. As mentioned above, single year of age data are available up to an open-ended category of 90 and over for all five Censuses considered here. The data are grouped into five-year age categories for the present analysis which, for the most part, utilizes the nine age groups from 50-54 to 90 and over.

Cohort. The above age data across the five census periods are used to delineate birth cohorts for five-year age groups by designating, for example, the 50-54 in 1940, 60-64 in 1950, 70-74 in 1960, 80-84 in 1970, and 90 and over in 1980 age groups as being a birth cohort (the period of birth being 1885-1889). The 50 and over populations' five-year age groups for 1940-1980 thus yields 17 period-of-birth cohorts, the birth periods being from "before 1850" to 1925-1929.

Period. The periods considered here are those of the five censuses, 1940, 1950, 1960, 1970, and 1980. Period, of course, will be a central concept in the examination of period-specific levels of migration/mobility and characteristics.

Sex and *Race.* The respondent's sex is designated for all years. Race is recodable into seven comparable categories across the five periods: (1) white, (2) black, (3)American Indian, (4) Japanese, (5) Chinese, (6) Filipino, and (7) other. In the present analysis, a white/nonwhite dichotomy is used.

Marital Status. From these data it is possible to obtain five mutually exclusive categories of marital status across censuses: (1) married, spouse present, (2) widowed, (3) divorced, (4) separated, (5) never-married. The literature indicates that the major substantive concern for migration/ mobility research is whether or not the respondent has a spouse present, and in the macro-level analyses of aggregate data this variable has therefore been recoded accordingly into the percent of respondents without a spouse present. However, for the micro-level analysis, four dummy variables, "married, spouse present", "widowed", "never-married", and "separated or divorced" are utilized.

Education. Level of educational attainment is included in the data for all years, and comparable categories in terms of single years of education from 0 to 16 years and more can be obtained. For the macro-level analyses, mean levels of education are used, and in the micro- level analyses, education is used as a continuous variable, ranging from 0 to 16 years and over.

Children Ever Born. The number of children ever born is included in the data from all five Censuses. In the case of the 50 years and over populations, this represents completed fertility. In the aggregate analyses, the mean number of children ever born is used, and in the micro-level analyses, this variable is retained in continuous form.

METHODS OF ANALYSIS

The tests of the hypotheses will be carried out using an aggregate data set created from the 1940 through 1980 Census Microdata Files. In addition to age, period, and cohort, the variables included in this data set are those utilized in the hypotheses, which are described above. All independent and dependent variables are age-specific for five year age groups for the fifty years old and older population. They are percent female, percent white, percent without spouse, mean years of completed education, mean number of children ever born, rates of interstate migration, and rates of local mobility.

First, analyses will be performed to determine whether or not significant age, period, and cohort effects on interstate migration and local mobility exist. Dummy variables will be computed for the nine age groups, the five periods, and the seventeen cohorts, and multiple regressions will be performed using each of the three sets of dummy variables in turn as independent variables in models using rates of interstate migration and rates of local mobility as dependent variables, respectively. This will be accomplished by estimating models of the general form:

$$Y = u + Eb_iX_i \quad \text{(eq. 1)}$$

The X_i are the dummy variables in each of the three sets for age, period, and cohort, and the Y is rates of interstate migration in one model and rates of local mobility in the other.

Following these initial analyses, the above-hypothesized relationships will be examined. If significant age, period, and cohort effects on interstate migration and local mobility are found to exist, each of the hypothesized relationships will be tested within age groups, periods, and groups of cohorts. The tests of the hypotheses will be accomplished by using bivariate regression to examine the relationship of each independent variable with rates of interstate migration, and rates of local mobility, the general form of the model being:

$$Y = u + bX \quad \text{(eq. 2)}$$

Following the completion of the tests of the hypotheses, a micro-level analysis will be undertaken in order to supplement the macro-level analyses, in hopes of further clarifying the aggregate level findings. The data utilized for these analyses will be the above-described 1940-1980 Census Public Use Sample Microdata Files.

Two basic models will be estimated by cohorts using multivariate regression. The first model, which will be estimated separately for the male and female populations, includes a dummy variable for being white, dummy variables for the marital status categories "married spouse present", "widowed", and "never married", and education, retained as a continuous variable, as independent variables.

The second micro model includes all of the independent variables from the first, plus the number of children ever born. It will, of course, be estimated for the female population only, by cohort. The general form of the model is the same as that in equation 1, above.

The dependent variables in the micro-level analyses for both interstate migration and local mobility are whether the respondent moved or did not move. Therefore, the well-known problems involved in estimating models with dichotomous dependent variables using normal ordinary least squares multiple regression techniques must be addressed here. In short, several assumptions of OLS regression are violated. The normality of disturbance terms assumption does not hold because the disturbance terms, like the dependent variable, take on only two values. The homoscedasticity of the disturbance term assumption does not hold because the values of the disturbance term depend on the independent variables. And, most importantly, the estimated values of the dependent variable may not lie between 0 and 1, which they must, of course, in a linear probability model. This latter problem is the one of real concern to the researcher attempting to estimate such a model.

The problem has most often been approached through the use of logit or probit regression, which constrains the predicted values to fall in the necessary range. However, due to problems with using much of the available logit regression software with large data sets or weighted data sets, an iterative method for using OLS regression to estimate models with dichotomous dependent variables has been developed by Randall Olsen (1980), Mitchell and Butler (1986) and others. Briefly, this statistical technique for the estimation of linear probability models is as follows: First, OLS multiple regression is used to estimate a linear probability of moving model. The predicted values PR1 generated by the probability of moving model are used to construct a weight WT1 defined as:

WT1 = 1 /(SQRT (PR1 * (1-PR1)))

This weight is applied to the linear probability function to correct for the heteroscedastic disturbance term. Because it is possible for the predicted probabilities to be less than 1 or exceed 0, any such predicted value is set equal to .5, minimizing their effects. This second step is iterated until convergence, i.e., until the regression coefficients stop changing.

This iterative technique is used in all of the micro-level regressions in this study. From a pragmatic standpoint, this approach is especially appropriate here because the data sets used are both quite large, and weighted.

IV. Results

This chapter contains three sections. First, the results of the analyses to determine the existence of significant age, period, and cohort effects on interstate migration and local mobility are presented and summarized. The second section presents and summarizes the results of the tests of the hypothesized relationships set forth in H1 through H10a above. Finally, the results of the supplementary micro-level analyses are presented and summarized.

RESULTS OF THE TESTS FOR AGE, PERIOD, AND COHORT EFFECTS

Tables 4 and 5 show the results of the multivariate analyses utilizing sets of dummy variables for age groups, periods, and cohorts, respectively, as independent variables. The dependent variable is the probability of engaging in interstate migration.

The results in Table 4 are from the multiple regression of age group dummy variables on rates of interstate migration. The age groups used as reference groups are 50-54, 65-69, and 90>, which are generally considered to be life cycle milestones. The periods included are 1960-1980, because preliminary analyses indicate that the inclusion of the two earliest periods nullifies any age effect that might exist. This regression yields an R^2 that indicates 44 percent of the variance in the dependent variable is explained at a level of significance of better than .05.

The second half of Table 4 shows the results of the regression of period dummy variables on rates of interstate migration. The R^2 is .63 and the period effect is highly significant.

Table 4: **THE EFFECTS OF AGE AND PERIOD ON RATES OF INTERSTATE MIGRATION FOR THE OLDER U.S. POPULATION: 1960-1980**

Age	B	Significance
55-59 Years	-.53889	.1272
60-64 Years	-.33889	.3288
70-74 Years	-.60556	.0889
75-79 Years	-1.13556	.0032
80-84 Years	-.93222	.0123
85-89 Years	-.47556	.1755
R^2 = .44072		.0482

Period	B	Significance
1940	-3.52667	.0000
1960	-2.46222	.0000
1970	-2.71222	.0000
1980	-1.87778	.0002
R^2 = .63345		.0000

Table 5:**THE COHORT EFFECT ON RATES OF INTERSTATE MIGRATION**
FOR THE OLDER U.S. POPULATION: 1940-1980

Cohort	B	Significance
1	.29500	.8891
2	-1.95500	.3078
3	-1.85500	.2135
4	-1.17500	.4271
5	.19167	.8826
6	.24167	.8523
7	.25750	.8304
8	-.00250	.9983
9	-.21100	.8532
10	.13500	.9106
11	.19500	.8711
12	-.50500	.6976
13	-.29500	.8203
14	-.08500	.9539
R^2 = .4324		.9772

In Table 5, the results of the regression to check for a significant cohort effect on interstate migration are presented. No such effect is found.

Tables 6-8 present the results from the estimation of regressions examining the effect of dummy variables for age groups, periods, and cohorts, respectively, on rates of local mobility.

The results of the regression to test the effect of age on local mobility rates in the first half of Table 6 are based on the elderly population (>65) in 1960-1980 only. The main focus of this study is the elderly population, and preliminary analyses indicate that the inclusion of the earlier periods and the non- elderly population nullify any age effect on local migration. The 65-69 age group serves as the reference group. The results show that coefficients are positive as would be expected with elderly local mobility, which increases at the oldest ages, and that the effect of age is significant.

The second half of Table 6 contains the results of the regression to test for a significant period effect, with 1950 as the reference period. The R^2 is quite high, and the effect of the period dummies on rates of local mobility is very highly significant.

Table 7 presents the results of the regression of the cohort dummy variables on rates of local mobility. These results indicate that a significant cohort effect does exist. Since the elderly population is the focus of this study, Table 8 presents the results of the regression to test for a cohort effect for the 65 and older population only. The R^2 is greatly increased in relation to that for the 50 and older population, and the level of significance is much higher.

RESULTS OF TESTS OF THE HYPOTHESES

Interstate Migration: H1-H5.

As indicated above, no significant effect of cohort on rates of interstate migration was found. Therefore, the relationships in H1-H5 are examined within age groups and periods.

Table 6: **THE EFFECT OF AGE AND PERIOD ON RATES OF LOCAL MOBILITY FOR THE ELDERLY U.S. POPULATION: 1960-1980**

Age	B	Significance
70-74 Years	.13333	.9610
75-79 Years	.74333	.7855
80-84 Years	2.82000	.3117
85-89 Years	6.06333	.0424
90 Years and Over	9.16333	.0050
R^2 = .61924		.0247

Period	B	Significance
1940	19.61111	.0000
1950	18.69667	.0000
1960	5.39556	.0006
1980	-1.82333	.2177
R^2 = .90748		.0000

Table   7:   **THE COHORT EFFECT ON RATES OF LOCAL MOBILITY FOR THE OLDER U.S. POPULATION**

Cohort	B	Significance
1	16.85500	.0717
2	21.39500	.0244
3	21.09500	.0052
4	21.74000	.0041
5	18.61500	.0051
6	17.54500	.0079
7	14.72500	.0151
8	14.24250	.0184
9	13.29300	.0202
10	9.01000	.1251
11	8.57750	.1435
12	2.34500	.7065
13	3.42833	.5824
14	-.08000	.9909

$R^2 = .52562$ .0230

Table 8. **THE COHORT EFFECT ON RATES OF LOCAL MOBILITY FOR THE ELDERLY U.S. POPULATION**

Cohort	B	Significance
1	12.82667	.0375
2	17.36667	.0073
3	17.06667	.0015
4	17.71167	.0011
5	14.58667	.0022
6	13.51667	.0038
7	7.78333	.0693
8	6.64667	.1158
9	2.11667	.6037
11	-3.42333	.4548
12	-4.59833	.3188
13	-5.87333	.3143
14	-5.79333	.3207

R^2 = .83276 .0000

Table 9 shows the results of the bivariate regressions of the independent variables and rates of interstate migration for the non-elderly (50-64 years), the young elderly (65-79 years), the old elderly (80-90>), and the total elderly population (65-90>), for 1960-1980. For the percent female, the regression coefficients and R^2s are weak and insignificant, for the most part, with the exception of the 66-79 age group, which has a positive and highly significant coefficient.

The percent white yields somewhat more interesting results, with all of the elderly age groups' coefficients being significant at the .05 level or higher, and the non-elderly age group's coefficient is significant at the .1 level or better. However, in every case, the direction of the relationships is the opposite of that hypothesized.

The results for the percent without a spouse are in the direction expected, with the exception of the old elderly age group. However, only the young elderly age group has a significant coefficient. The last two variables, education and number of children ever born, in all but one case yield coefficients in the direction predicted, but, none are significant at the .05 level.

Table 10 presents the results of the tests of the hypothesized relationships within each of the five periods, 1940-1980. For the percent white, there is no pattern to the direction of the coefficients, and the only two significant coefficients have opposite signs. All but one of the coefficients for percent white are statistically significant, but only one is in the direction predicted. The percent without a spouse yields a significant coefficient for 1960 only, and there is no apparent pattern to the direction of the coefficients. One of the coefficients for education is significant, and it is one of the two that are in the expected direction. With children ever born, the results show only one significant coefficient, and no discernable pattern in the directions of the coefficients.

Local Mobility: H6-H10a.

As indicated above, significant effects of age, period, and cohorts on rates of local mobility were found. Therefore, the relationships in H6-H10a are examined within age groups, cohorts and periods.

Table 9: **THE RESULTS OF TESTS OF HYPOTHESES ADDRESSING THE RELATIONSHIP OF FIVE INDEPENDENT VARIABLES AND RATES OF INTERSTATE MIGRATION FOR THE OLDER U.S. POPULATION, 1940-1980; WITHIN AGE GROUPS**

Percent Female	R^2	B	Significance
50-64 Years	.01999	.09423	.7168
65-79 Years	.17642	-.11493	.2604
80-90 Years	.64292	.11805	.0093
65-90 Years	.04766	.02756	.3841

Percent White	R^2	B	Significance
50-64 Years	.37071	-.24922	.0818
65-79 Years	.46675	-.33723	.0425
80-90 Years	.44631	-.23185	.0492
65-90 Years	.42088	-.26623	.0036

Percent Without Spouse	R^2	B	Significance
50-64 Years	.04716	-.0351	.5746
65-79 Years	.71268	-.06600	.0042
80-90 Years	.36364	.04957	.24727
65-90 Years	.00324	-.00197	.8225

Education	R^2	B	Significance
50-64 Years	.14597	.21329	.3102
65-79 Years	.28973	.37334	.1349
80-90 Years	.16434	.34303	.2790
65-90 Years	.17323	.28299	.0858

Children Ever Born	R^2	B	Significance
50-64 Years	.15850	.92215	.2886
65-79 Years	.10592	-.51305	.3928
80-90 Years	.22983	-.54664	.1916
65-90 Years	.11809	-.42888	.1626

Table 10: **THE RESULTS OF TESTS OF HYPOTHESES ADDRESSING THE RELATIONSHIPS OF FIVE INDEPENDENT VARIABLES AND RATES OF INTERSTATE MIGRATION FOR THE OLDER U.S. POPULATION, 1940-1980; WITHIN PERIODS**

Percent Female	R^2	B	Significance
1940	.42189	.11210	.7168
1950	.38214	-.31351	.0760
1960	.21136	-.04540	.2131
1970	.05565	.02575	.5411
1980	.02634	-.01267	.6765

Percent White	R^2	B	Significance
1940	.83092	-.20170	.0006
1950	.56807	.60619	.0190
1960	.51076	-.20837	.0305
1970	.45152	-.28471	.0283
1980	.06250	-.09260	.5165

Percent Without Spouse	R^2	B	Significance
1940	.03394	.00618	.6351
1950	.28606	-.03971	.1379
1960	.39524	-.01129	.0697
1970	.06107	.00525	.5215
1980	.02745	-.00366	.6701

Education	R^2	B	Significance
1940	.03733	-.26898	.6184
1950	.24133	1.36012	.1793
1960	.4333	.31916	.0539
1970	.01873	-.06679	.7255
1980	.03832	.09798	.6137

Children Ever Born	R^2	B	Significance
1940	.03477	.33424	.6309
1950	.09107	-1.36904	.4300
1960	.43103	-.53733	.0548
1970	.01090	.21005	.7893
1980	.02152	.32875	.7056

Table 11: **THE RESULTS OF TESTS OF HYPOTHESES ADDRESSING THE RELATIONSHIPS OF FIVE INDEPENDENT VARIABLES AND RATES OF LOCAL MOBILITY FOR THE OLDER U.S. POPULATION, 1940–1980; WITHIN AGE GROUPS**

Percent Female	R^2	B	Significance
50-64 Years	.62090	-4.25340	.0117
65-79 Years	.40765	-.85606	.0642
80-90 Years	.00582	-.06723	.8454
65-90 Years	.12958	.32517	.1423

Percent White	R^2	B	Significance
50-64 Years	.20933	1.51659	.2156
65-79 Years	.62906	1.91834	.0108
80-90 Years	.28260	-1.10451	.1408
65-90 Years	.01911	.40584	.5844

Percent Without Spouse	R^2	B	Significance
50-64 Years	.00084	-.03300	.9410
65-79 Years	.05066	.08622	.5604
80-90 Years	.61713	.38662	.0121
65-90 Years	.53554	-.18609	.0003

Education	R^2	B	Significance
50-64 Years	.52394	-3.27237	.0275
65-79 Years	.86174	-3.15495	.0003
80-90 Years	.61992	-3.98850	.0118
65-90 Years	.73463	-4.16962	.0000

Children Ever Born	R^2	B	Significance
50-64 Years	.04076	-3.78688	.6024
65-79 Years	.93694	7.47697	.0000
80-90 Years	.48426	4.75031	.0373
65-90 Years	.66652	7.29013	.0000

Table 11 contains the results of the bivariate regressions of the independent variables on local mobility rates within age groups. The age groups 50-54 (the non-elderly), 65-79 (the younger elderly), 80-90> (the oldest elderly), and 65-90> (the entire elderly population) are used here.

For percent female, the coefficients are mostly in the opposite direction from that expected. Only the overall elderly age group shows a positive coefficient, and it is
not one of the two that are significant.

The coefficients for the percent white are in the direction hypothesized, with the exception of that for the oldest elderly age group. However, the youngest elderly age group produces the only significant coefficient.

The results for the percent without spouse are quite interesting. The elderly age groups all show coefficients in the expected direction. Furthermore, the non-elderly age group has a weak negative and highly insignificant coefficient, and the coefficients become positive and more significant with each older age group. All of the elderly age groups show coefficients that are in the direction hypothesized, and the oldest elderly and overall elderly groups' coefficients are highly significant.

For education, the coefficients for all age groups are in the direction expected, and all are significant. The highest levels of significance are associated with the elderly age groups. The coefficients for children ever born are in the expected direction and significant for all of the elderly age groups, with those for the youngest elderly and the overall elderly groups being very highly significant.

Table 12 contains the results of the bivariate regressions of the independent variables and local mobility within periods. In terms of the hypothesized relationships, the coefficients for most of the independent variables exhibit some interesting patterns across time.

The relationship of percent female was expected to be positive. These results show that beginning in the earliest period, 1940, the coefficients change from being negative and significant, to negative and insignificant, to positive and insignificant, to positive and significant, and finally, in 1980, to positive and highly significant. That is, throughout the entire period of the study, the coefficients have moved in the direction of being more and more positive and significant.

Table 12: **THE RESULTS OF TESTS OF HYPOTHESES ADDRESSING THE RELATIONSHIPS OF FIVE INDEPENDENT VARIABLES AND RATES OF LOCAL MOBILITY FOR THE OLDER U.S. POPULATION, 1940-1980; WITHIN PERIODS**

Percent Female	R^2	B	Significance
1940	.77304	-.58338	.0018
1950	.06851	-.19368	.4963
1960	.24177	.30716	.1788
1970	.53885	.53201	.0243
1980	.65976	.42151	.0078

Percent White	R^2	B	Significance
1940	.27887	.44921	.1439
1950	.07019	-.31088	.4909
1960	.49907	-1.30289	.0334
1970	.03155	-.46569	.6475
1980	.21333	1.13750	.2107

Percent Without Spouse	R^2	B	Significance
1940	.81244	-.11621	.0009
1950	.13204	-.03936	.3364
1960	.09082	.03422	.4306
1970	.56095	.10565	.0202
1980	.65549	.11840	.0082

Education	R^2	B	Significance
1940	.79797	4.78072	.0012
1950	.35072	2.39232	.0929
1960	.00217	.14284	.9050
1970	.29443	-1.75814	.1312
1980	.44435	-2.21810	.0042

Children Ever Born	R^2	B	Significance
1940	.82750	-6.26827	.0007
1950	.35529	-3.94535	.0930
1960	.01816	.69765	.7296
1970	.50568	9.13456	.0317
1980	.13462	5.46732	.3314

For percent white, no pattern is discernable. Only two of the coefficients are in the expected direction, and the positive coefficients are found at the earliest and most recent time periods. The only significant coefficient is for 1960, and it is negative.

The coefficients for the percent without spouse exhibit a pattern similar to that of percent white. That is, the coefficients move on a continuum from being negative and highly significant in 1940 to being positive and significant, and positive and highly significant in 1960 and 1980, respectively. Again, the most recent periods produce the coefficients in the direction hypothesized.

The same pattern can be observed for education. The expected direction of the coefficients for education is negative. These results show that they change continuously from being positive and highly significant in 1940 to being negative and highly significant in 1980, with only the two most recent periods' coefficients being in the expected direction.

Essentially the same pattern can be observed for children ever born. The coefficients move constantly from being negative and highly significant in 1940, toward being more positive, the expected direction, with only the two most recent periods, again, showing coefficients in the hypothesized direction.

Table 13 shows the results of the bivariate regressions of the independent variables and rates of local mobility within birth cohort groups. The cohorts are grouped first into three groups containing five cohorts each: cohorts 1-5, cohorts 6-10, and cohorts 11-15; and then into two groups: cohorts 1-9, and cohorts 10-17.

For percent female, the results for the three cohort groups result in significant coefficients for each group, with the least significant coefficient being for the most recent group of cohorts. The two-group division shows this even more clearly, with the least recent cohorts yielding a highly significant coefficient and coefficient for the most recent cohorts being significant at the .10 level. However, the direction of the coefficients in every case is negative; the opposite of that expected. Although the strengthening of the hypothesized positive relationship obviously does not occur, the negative relationship does weaken with more recent cohort membership.

For percent white, the coefficients for all cohort groups are positive, as expected. However, the most significant coefficient and the greatest in magnitude in both the three- and two-group divisions is for the most recent cohorts. This is not the hypothesized cohort effect.

Table 13: **THE RESULTS OF TESTS OF HYPOTHESES ADDRESSING THE EFFECT OF COHORT MEMBERSHIP ON THE RELATIONSHIPS OF FIVE INDEPENDENT VARIABLES AND RATES OF LOCAL MOBILITY FOR THE OLDER U.S. POPULATION, 1940-1980**

Percent Female

Cohorts	R^2	B	Significance
1-5	.50201	-.41503	.0326
6-10	.55261	-.96220	.0002
11-15	.26874	-.91961	.0575
1-9	.47488	-.82404	.0001
10-17	.13653	-.59342	.1088

Percent White

Cohorts	R^2	B	Significance
1-5	.24335	.37077	.1772
6-10	.02101	1.07421	.5421
11-15	.1521	3.49366	.1679
1-9	.00438	.18250	.7533
10-17	.18566	2.52305	.0579

Percent Without Spouse

Cohorts	R^2	B	Significance
1-5	.15127	-.09233	.3009
6-10	.50375	-.30092	.0005
11-15	.17471	-.22625	.1370
1-9	.18729	-.15298	.0307
10-17	.06443	-.11991	.2802

Table 13 (cont.)

Education

Cohorts	R^2	B	Significance
1-5	.02532	1.377	.6826
6-10	.13987	-7.555	.1043
11-15	.1936	-4.625	.1153
1-9	.17071	-5.41974	.0401
10-17	.21318	-3.60302	.0404

Children Ever Born

Cohorts	R^2	B	Significance
1-5	.07801	-3.49333	.4667
6-10	.13074	9.38634	.1172
11-15	.30958	29.23546	.0388
1-9	.15055	6.48915	.0553
10-17	.13081	12.27506	.1171

The coefficients for the effect of percent without spouse on local mobility rates are in the opposite direction as that hypothesized. The coefficients for the two-group division indicate that the most significant negative effect of this variable is for the least recent cohorts. The pattern of significance is not as clear for the three group division.

For education, the coefficients are all negative, as expected, except for the cohort 1-5 group in the three- group division, which is positive, but the lowest in magnitude and least significant of all of the coefficients. The cohorts 6-10 and 11-15 groups indicate much higher and more significant negative relationships, and the coefficients for the two- group division are both negative and significant. These results indicate that the negative relationship between education and rates of local mobility is somewhat weaker for more recent cohorts, as expected.

The coefficients for children ever born are in the expected direction for all of the cohort groupings except the cohorts 1-5 group. The three-group division shows a pattern of movement from a negative and insignificant coefficient for the cohorts 1-5 group to positive and significant, the expected direction, for the cohorts 11-15 group.

RESULTS OF THE MICRO-LEVEL ANALYSES

As indicated above, the 1940-1980 U.S. Census Public Use Sample microdata files are used to estimate models that include all of the independent variables from the aggregate level analysis. In these analyses there are three separate dummy variables for marital status: widowed, married, spouse present, and never- married. Since these results are presented for the female and male populations separately, the percent female is not used as an independent variable. As previously explained, a multiple regression technique is used in estimating these probability models, the dependent variables being the probability of engaging in interstate migration or local mobility. These analyses are done from a cohort perspective, and Tables 14-16 show results for cohorts 5, 7, 9, 11, 13, and 15, number 5 being the 1865-1869 birth cohort and number 15 the 1915-1919 birth cohort.

Elderly Cohort Migration Patterns

Table 14: **RESULTS OF THE MULTIVARIATE REGRESSION OR FIVE
          INDEPENDENT VARIABLES WITH THE PROBABILITY OF
          ENGAGING IN INTERSTATE MIGRATION FOR THE FEMALE
          AND MALE OLDER U.S. POPULATIONS; WITHIN COHORTS**

FEMALES

Cohort	R^2	White	Widowed	Married Spouse Present	Never Married	Education
5	.01233	-.01211	.02059	.01633	.00422	.00455
7	.01500	.01719	.03272	-.00387	.05735	.00239
9	.00662	.02153	.00375	-.01503	-.00663	.00222
11	.00343	.00924	.01827	.01717	.02452	.00200
13	.00670	.01931	-.02452	-.03826	-.03616	.00299
15	.00714	.01345	-.00240	-.00732	-.03758	.00419

MALES

Cohort	R^2	White	Widowed	Married Spouse Present	Never Married	Education
5	.00846	-.00399	.00700	-.00894	-.02439	.00273
7	.01952	-.06496	.00146	-.03358	.00657	-.41E-3
9	.00439	.27E-3	-.01067	-.02055	-.01040	.00277
11	.00447	.02457	-.03308	-.03909	-.05970	.36E-3
13	.00815	.01530	-.04834	-.05517	-.06247	.00235
15	.01246	.03860	-.02391	-.04606	-.04966	.00537

Table 15: **RESULTS OF THE MULTIVARIATE REGRESSION OR FIVE INDEPENDENT VARIABLES WITH THE PROBABILITY OF ENGAGING IN LOCAL MOBILITY FOR THE FEMALE AND MALE OLDER U.S. POPULATIONS; WITHIN COHORTS**

FEMALES

Cohort	R^2	White	Widowed	Married Spouse Present	Never Married	Education
5	.04115	-.17357	-.15558	-.24752	-.26071	-.01283
7	.01480	-.08319	-.24516	-.25319	-.17689	-.95E-3
9	.01070	-.08667	-.14771	-.11199	-.13888	-.00471
11	.00904	-.04883	-.01495	-.08008	-.03419	-.24E-3
13	.00759	-.02132	-.07027	-.09020	-.08553	-.00623
15	.01593	.02024	-.01035	-.10382	-.08882	-.00497

MALES

Cohort	R^2	White	Widowed	Married Spouse Present	Never Married	Education
5	.05869	-.23715	-.07927	-.21483	.00243	-.00599
7	.01476	-.03316	-.25311	-.22580	-.17489	-.48E-3
9	.00730	-.12090	-.07318	-.04713	.53E-3	-.98E-3
11	.01418	-.03990	-.02493	-.10774	-.05795	-.00387
13	.00368	-.02087	-.06712	-.07531	-.11831	-.77E-3
15	.01070	-.02141	-.18961	-.15303	-.11784	-.69E-3

Table   16:   **RESULTS OF THE MULITVARIATE REGRESSIONS OF SIX INDEPENDENT VARIABLES WITH THE PROBABILITY OF ENGAGING IN INTERSTATE MIGRATION, AND WITH THE PROBABILITY OF ENGAGING IN LOCAL MOBILITY; FOR THE OLDER FEMALE U.S. POPULATION WITHIN COHORTS**

INTERSTATE MIGRATION

Cohort	R^2	White	Widowed	Married Spouse Present	Never Married	Education	Children Ever Born
5	.01357	-.01357	.02733	.02115		.00568	.00226
7	.01289	.01314	.02808	-.00773	.03081	.00317	.00300
9	.00751	.01975	.00372	-.01478	-.03446	.00195	-.00168
11	.00370	.01079	.01756	.01672	.00370	.00155	-.00219
13	.00871	.01529	-.02433	-.03789	-.03117	.00410	.00286
15	.00811	.01347	-.00241	-.00730	-.03750	.00418	-3.30E-5

LOCAL MOBILITY

Cohort	R^2	White	Widowed	Married Spouse Present	Never Married	Education	Children Ever Born
5	.05415	-.16000	-.13440	-.22974	·	-.01079	.01851
7	.01548	-.09295	-.24517	-.25266	-.19959	-7.98E-4	-.00360
9	.01059	-.08593	-.14780	-.11196	-.15976	-.00412	1.18E-4
11	.00996	-.04471	-.01493	-.08026	-.08630	-9.20E-4	-.00338
13	.00750	-.02128	-.06985	-.08988	-.09744	-.00617	-.00186
15	.01695	.02117	-.00973	-.10434	-.07671	-.00423	.00586

Table 14 presents the results of the regression of being white, widowed, married with spouse present, never married, and years of completed education on the probability of engaging in interstate migration. No cohort analyses were performed using the aggregate data for interstate migration due to the lack of a significant cohort effect. Although the aggregate-level measures of the independent variables generally were not effective in explaining the rates of elderly interstate migration, estimating the micro-level models will make it possible to examine the hypothesized relationships from an individual perspective. Thus any differences in the performance of the independent variables from these two methodological approaches can be observed. The coefficients for being white show the same pattern for both the male and female populations. That is, overall, the directions are as hypothesized, with the earliest cohorts having negative coefficients. The coefficients for being widowed show a similar pattern for men and women, with both being positive at the earliest cohorts, and changing to the hypothesized direction for more recent cohorts, with the change in direction occurring at cohort 9 for the men, but not until cohort 13 for the women. Education shows a positive relationship with the propensity to migrate interstate for all cohorts, both sexes, as hypothesized, with the exception of the males, cohort 7.

Table 15 presents the results of the above model for the female and male populations using the probability of local mobility as the dependent variable. There is a great deal of consistency in the results for the females and the males. For being white, the coefficients are negative (the opposite as that hypothesized) in every case except for females, cohort 15. The coefficients for being widowed are negative in every case for both men and women (the hypothesized direction was positive). Education shows a negative relationship with the propensity to move locally in every case for both sexes, as hypothesized.

The second model utilized for these micro- level analyses is identical to the first, with the exception that the number of children ever born is added as an independent variable. This model is estimated for the female population using the probability of migrating interstate and the probability of moving locally as dependent variables, and the results presented in the two sections of Table 16. These results for the variables included in the first model are essentially the same as those for the female population found in Tables 14 and 15. With regard to the number of children ever born, the results are not as expected. No discernable pattern in the direction of the relationships of this variable with either interstate migration or local mobility is apparent.

V. Discussion

The most often noted deficiency in studies of elderly migration/mobility is the lack of a theoretical framework. The fact that there are no well-established theoretical perspectives in this area has become a self-perpetuating situation. The "theoretical" articles that appear are nonempirical and in the form of a lament of the dearth of elderly migration theories, combined with a call for research that will move us in the direction of such theoretical development. The empirical studies that are done, however, continue to avoid addressing the issue for the most part. Research efforts during the early stages of development of an area of inquiry often consist largely of studies that seek to establish empirical regularities with regard to relationships between the phenomena of interest and their possible determinants. However, it is also important for social scientists to address the primary issue of the state of theoretical development.

A review of some of the most-widely cited literature in the areas of elderly migration and local mobility indicates that a vast majority of the work has been cross-sectional, using traditional methodologies. In fact, the methodological approach most often taken involves tabulating variables thought to be related to elderly migration/mobility. Those studies, in effect, examine an age-effect within a single period. And from the available literature in this relatively recent area of investigation it is almost impossible to compare similar cross-sectional studies done at different periods (nearly all of the studies to be found in the literature utilize 1960 or 1970 data, most often from the U.S. Census). Furthermore, the few longitudinal studies cited as exceptions, as a rule, only involve two periods, and examine trends in variables' effects for a single decade. Often, conclusions of a general nature regarding the dynamics of elderly migration and local mobility have been drawn from the findings of these studies.

The question which must be asked, of course, is whether the relationships observed in recent cross- sectional studies hold across time. This is, in effect, to ask whether generalizations regarding these observed relationships are valid. Although there are problems regarding the ambiguity of the results of the present analyses involving elderly interstate migration as the dependent variable, and there are distinct differences in the analytical approaches used in the various studies, the present findings regarding period effects of the independent variables on elderly local mobility do have some interesting implications for the validity issue.

ELDERLY INTERSTATE MIGRATION

The results of the tests of the hypotheses regarding elderly interstate migration, H1-H5, are, for the most part, ambiguous and unsupportive. Looking at the results of the regressions within age groups, for percent female, only the 80-90> age group shows a significant positive effect, as predicted. The percent white has negative significant coefficients, the opposite of the hypothesized direction, for all age groups except the non- elderly, which is also negative, but only at the .08 level of significance. For percent without spouse, the only significant coefficient is for the younger elderly, and it is in the direction predicted. The coefficients for educational attainment and children ever born are in the hypothesized directions for all of the elderly age groups, but none of them are significant.

The tests of the elderly interstate migration hypotheses within periods are not unlike those just described. For percent female, none of the periods have significant coefficients in the hypothesized direction. Percent white has a significant positive coefficient for the 1950 period only. Percent without spouse and educational attainment have significant coefficients in the expected direction for only one period, in each case. And children ever born indicates no significant relationship in any period.

The results for percent without spouse are possibly interpretable in terms of assertions derived from the findings of the elderly migration research to date. The younger segment of the elderly population is shown to have a negative and highly significant relationship between this variable and interstate migration rates, as expected, while the coefficient within the oldest segment of the elderly population is positive and insignificant. Past studies do indicate that the oldest elderly engage in long distance migration for entirely different reasons than the younger segment. Specifically, such mobility by the former group is often return migration for health and assistance reasons. It would stand to reason that a majority of these migrants would be female and widows. This contention is also supported by the results of the percent female analysis within age groups, in that the only positive significant coefficient is for the oldest segment of the elderly population. However, this does not explain the fact that the percent without spouse has a very weak and insignificant coefficient for the total elderly population, which is contradictory to all previous findings.

Overall, the results regarding H1-H5 are ambiguous and insignificant, and these hypotheses appear to be unsupported by these analyses. It must be concluded that we cannot explain elderly interstate migration very well with models based on variables derived from much of the literature in this area.

ELDERLY LOCAL MOBILITY

As indicated above, the work to date in the area of elderly migration/mobility leads us to expect that local movers should be predominately female, white, without a spouse, of lower education, and have fewer children than nonmovers. The tests of hypotheses H6-H10, which relate to elderly local mobility, within age groups produce some interesting results.

The first two variables, percent female, and percent white, are the characteristics represented in hypotheses 6 and 7. In the case of the former, only one coefficient, that for the overall elderly age group, is in the hypothesized direction and it is insignificant. In the latter case, the coefficient for the 65- 79 age group is positive, strong, and significant, as expected. The coefficient for the oldest elderly age group is negative, although insignificant. Most past studies have not involved a great deal of age detail within the 65 and over population, and this change in direction could be explained in part by the white/black mortality "crossover" at the oldest ages, when local mobility increases.

Since larger proportions of blacks survive to the oldest elderly ages relative to whites, and it is at these ages that local mobility is most likely to occur, the observed change in direction of the effect of being white on local mobility within the oldest age group is not completely surprising. However, although the coefficient for percent white within the overall elderly age group is in the expected direction, it is insignificant, obviously due to the opposite signs for the two overall elderly age group components. In short, hypothesis 6 is not supported by this part of the analysis, and only partial support is found for hypothesis 7.

The characteristics central to hypotheses 8, 9, and 10 are percent without spouse, education, and children ever born. The coefficients for percent without spouse are in the hypothesized direction for all of the elderly age groups, with the oldest elderly group and the overall elderly groups' coefficients being highly significant. Again, one would expect the oldest elderly to show a stronger, more significant relationship for this variable than the younger elderly age group. And, the overall elderly group has the most significant coefficient of all, which is consistent with the findings from the literature.

Within all of the elderly age groups, the coefficients for education and children ever born are in the directions hypothesized (negative for the former and positive for the latter), and highly significant. Therefore, strong support for hypotheses 8-10 is found in the analysis which tests their effects within age groups.

These results are especially interesting because the age groups involve people of the same ages from five periods covering a fifty year span. The indication is that there may be some basis for making more general statements regarding the effect of widowhood, education, and number of children on the elderly's propensity to move locally. Therefore, some of the conclusions found in much of the literature are supported here. However, an equally important implication stems from the large number of generalizations from the literature that do not find support in this analysis, the point being that longitudinal investigations are necessary to establish the validity of such assertions.

The present findings concerning the effects of these variables for five periods covering a span of fifty years exhibit some interesting patterns. Regarding the percent female, the relationship with elderly local mobility is positive and significant, as expected, for the two most recent periods. However, this is not the case for all five periods examined. In 1940, the earliest period included, the relationship is negative, strong, and highly significant. In 1950 it is negative, weak, and insignificant. And in 1960 it is positive and insignificant.

The relationship of percent white with elderly local mobility is positive as expected for the 1980 period. However from 1950-1970 it is negative. And in 1960-1980 the direction of this relationship changes from being significantly negative to weakly negative, and finally positive in the most recent period only.

The present analysis shows the relationship of percent without spouse present and elderly local mobility to be significantly positive, as expected, in 1970 and 1980 only. In 1940 this relationship is negative, very strong, and highly significant. In 1950 it is weakly negative. And in 1960 it is positive, but weak and insignificant.

The relationship of educational attainment and elderly local mobility is shown by the present analysis to be positive, strong and highly significant in 1940, positive in 1950, and very weak and positive in 1960. It is only in 1970 that this relationship becomes negative, and only in the most recent period that it is significantly so.

Similarly, the number of children ever born is strong, negative, and highly significant in 1940, less strong and negative in 1950, and weak, positive and insignificant in 1960. Only in 1970 does it become significantly positive, as hypothesized.

This analysis involving the relationships of the independent variables and elderly local mobility within periods lend at least partial support to hypotheses 6-10, in that the more recent periods indicate significant relationships in the expected directions. It is pointed out below that the difference in the results across periods and the pattern of change in these results are of interest in and of themselves with regard to the above-mentioned validity of generalizations issue, and the implications for the directions of future research which should seek to investigate the factors underlying such patterns of change.

Based on the results of the tests of those hypotheses concerned with elderly local mobility performed within age groups and within periods, there appears to be little support for the hypothesized relationships of percent female and percent white. However, there is considerable support for the hypothesized relationships of percent without spouse, education, and children ever born with elderly local mobility. It can also be pointed out that based on the analyses discussed so far, overall, the variables derived from the literature appear to be far more effective in explaining elderly local mobility than elderly interstate migration.

A great deal of emphasis has been placed on the cohort perspective in the present study. The question that arises regarding this methodological orientation is: What does it add to our understanding, or, what can it tell us that looking at data for several periods in a more traditional manner cannot? The cohort perspective points out that cohort effects are largely due to the fact that the effects of certain life course events on demographic/social phenomena are ongoing once those events have occurred. Therefore, although these cohort effects may be mitigated by other circumstances, they follow cohort members throughout their lifetimes, to some degree. Thus the cohort orientation, in the present context, is not just a way of examining the stability of the relationships of demographic and social characteristics and elderly migration and local mobility across time. This perspective could ultimately allow us to understand period changes in terms of the process of cohort succession, which plays an important part in creating the age-specific period effects.

The subhypotheses that are associated with H6-H10, the elderly local mobility hypotheses, utilize groups of cohorts as the units of analysis. Hypotheses 6a-10a posit expected mitigating effects of cohort membership on the relationships of the independent variables and elderly local mobility.

Subhypothesis 6a predicts a strengthening of a positive relationship of percent female with elderly local mobility with more recent cohort membership. In a sense, this hypothesis is supported by the results of the cohort analysis in that, even though the coefficients for earlier and more recent groups of cohorts are negative, the more recent cohorts show weak and insignificant coefficients. This pattern of change from earlier to more recent cohorts is consistent with the observed pattern of change in the period effects on the relationship of these variables, which moved from being significantly negative in 1940 to being significantly positive in 1980.

The cohort results regarding percent white indicate relationships in the predicted direction in each case. However, the coefficients are not significant, and those for more recent cohorts are more strongly positive than those for earlier cohorts, the opposite of H7a's expectation. Although this hypothesis is not supported by the cohort analysis, the results are consistent with the direction of change in the coefficients found in the results of the analysis for this variable done within periods, which show a negative relationship at earlier periods, and a positive relationship for the most recent period.

The results of H8a, which addresses the effect of cohort

membership on the relationship of percent without spouse and elderly local mobility, are supportive of the hypothesis. Although the coefficients are negative, not as hypothesized, the earlier cohorts have strong significant coefficients, while those for the most recent cohorts are insignificant. This is also consistent with the direction of change observed in the period analysis of this variable, which showed a significant negative relationship in the earliest period and a pattern of change to significant positive coefficients in the most recent periods.

Education, when analyzed from a cohort perspective in the test of H9a, yields results that support this hypothesis. The direction of the coefficients is negative, as expected, and the negative effect is somewhat weaker for more recent cohorts. These findings also indicate a weak positive relationship for the group of earliest cohorts, and negative relationships for the two more recent groups. This is consistent with the period analysis pattern of change regarding this variable, which moved from being positive and significant in 1940 to being negative and significant in 1980.

H10a finds strong support in the cohort analysis of children ever born and elderly local mobility. The results indicate that this relationship is negative for the earliest group of cohorts, positive for the middle group, and much more strongly positive and significant for the most recent group of cohorts. Again, this perspective sheds some light on the period findings for children ever born, with the earliest periods producing significant negative coefficients, and a pattern of change being observed with positive coefficients for the most recent periods.

THE MICRO-LEVEL ANALYSES

The results of the supplementary micro- level analysis of the effects of the independent variables on local mobility should be discussed briefly. As indicated above, these analyses were performed within the same groups of cohorts utilized in the aggregate analyses, for the female and male populations. The analyses of the first micro model generally is consistent with the results of the aggregate cohort analyses, in terms of the direction and patterns in the magnitude of the coefficients for being a widow, and educational attainment. Although the coefficients for being white are negative, for the most part, their magnitude becomes smaller for the more recent cohorts, and, for the female population, the most recent cohort's coefficient is positive. The estimation of the second model, which is identical to the first with the exception that children ever born is added as an independent variable, results in very little change in the findings from the first micro model. However, the results for children ever born are ambiguous, with no discernable pattern in the signs of the coefficients. It is possible that the confounding effects of the other variables in the model are responsible.

It is of passing interest here that the results of the micro-level cohort analysis of the independent variables and interstate migration produced findings much more consistent with the hypotheses than those from the aggregate analyses. The relationships of all variables included in the micro models were on the whole in the hypothesized directions, with the exception of children ever born. The basic problem with practically all of these micro level findings and those in the models examining local mobility is the low R^2s and the small magnitude of the coefficients. This means that only a small amount of the variation in the dependent variable is being explained by the models, and that the direction of very small coefficients must be interpreted with caution because the large sample sizes will result in high levels of significance, even if coefficients are close to zero.

CONCLUSIONS

The obvious and repeated patterns that are evident in the findings from the analysis of the period effect on the associations of the independent variables and local mobility cannot be ignored, and the implications for the generalizability of the findings of many of the studies constituting the elderly migration/mobility literature must be recognized. In short, the relationships of each of the above variables, which have been utilized repeatedly in cross-sectional studies of elderly local mobility, observed in the analysis of data from only 40-50 years ago, are in the opposite direction of that expected from the recent literature. Even more interesting is the pattern of constant change in the magnitude and direction in the relationships of each of these variables with elderly local mobility, as they move toward the expected direction until, in the most recent periods, they are observed to be as expected.

It is noted above that the vast majority of the studies to date in this area utilize data from these more recent periods. These findings indicate that there may well be problems with generalizing from the findings of elderly migration/ mobility studies that are based on data from only one, or even two, recent periods.

It is recognized here that there are alternative explanations for the observed patterns of change in the effects of these independent variables across time on elderly mobility. One possible explanation involves methodological problems in previous studies. Another relates to the inadequate theoretical understanding of this phenomenon. Both of these explanations have been discussed above. However, further investigations are necessary before anything conclusive can be asserted regarding the validity of the above-mentioned generalizations because it is entirely possible that the patterns of change observed in the present analysis are a result of measurement error.

The same kinds of questions can be raised about the conclusions drawn in studies to date regarding the age effect on elderly migration/mobility. The present analyses indicate that, for the last thirty years of the total period covered, the age effects do appear to be as set forth in the literature. That is, for interstate migration, the data indicate that migration activity is highest at the normal retirement ages and at the oldest ages. For elderly local mobility, significant positive effects of age are found at the two oldest age groups, with the 90> group having the strongest and most significant coefficient.

An examination of the elderly migration/mobility literature indicates that a great many of the most often cited studies in this area utilize the same list of characteristics in describing the proportions of migrants and local movers that possess certain demographic and social characteristics. In line with the concerns raised above regarding whether the most constructive directions are being pursued in ongoing elderly migration/mobility research, in terms of what is needed to bring us closer to the beginnings of much needed development of theory in these areas, another question must be raised. How effective are the characteristics of elderly migrants and local movers repeatedly described in the literature, when included in models designed to explain or predict migration and mobility behavior in the elderly population as a whole? It is often the case that the variables available for use in a study are limited by the characteristics of the readily available data. However, after repeated failures to explain the variations encountered, it is necessary to evaluate the theoretical utility of these variables and their potential for future research.

The methodological approach used in the present study is more consistent with a model designed to explain or predict behavior than the descriptive approach most often taken in past elderly migration/mobility research. That is, the older population as a whole is taken to be the universe and the effects of social and demographic characteristics, used as independent variables, on the propensity to move within this population are estimated.   There are basic differences in this approach and that taken in most of the elderly migration/mobility studies to date, as described above.   To reiterate, the descriptive approach usually treats elderly movers as the universe of interest.   Then proportions of elderly movers bearing selected characteristics are described, and conclusions drawn based on the findings. The difference in what the findings of these two types of methodological approaches can tell us may be summarized in the following manner. The latter approach can indicate that a high proportion of long-distance elderly migrants, for example, are female and have higher than average educational attainment. The former approach can demonstrate the effect that being a female or having a higher than average level of educational attainment has on the propensity to engage in long distance migration. Obviously, just because most migrants are female, does not mean that most females migrate.   In fact, elderly mobility is a relatively rare event, especially long distance migration, with elderly interstate migration typically ranging from two to six or seven percent of the eligible population. However, if the characteristics of elderly movers derived from the literature are to be useful in models designed to investigate possible determinants of elderly mobility behavior, at least the expected direction of the relationships should hold.   If not, the models developed from the literature simply do not have much predictive or explanatory value.

A major finding of the present study is the difference in the effectiveness of the independent variables in models utilizing elderly interstate migration and elderly local mobility as dependent variables. This is evidenced by the fact that practically no support is indicated for the first five hypotheses. This discovery should not be especially surprising. One thing that has been established by the studies in the elderly migration/mobility literature is that an essential difference exists between the nature of elderly long-distance migration, and elderly local mobility. In fact, one of the specific asserted differences finds support in the present study, i.e., the relationships of age and these two types of elderly mobility.

More generally, it has been posited that long- distance elderly migration is more discretionary in nature, often involving moves for environmental amenities and quality of life reasons, as opposed to elderly local mobility which has been characterized as often being involuntary and assistance-oriented. If long distance elderly migration is indeed more discretionary, it is not surprising that it may well be more difficult to predict than local mobility. It has been asserted that the elderly interstate migration phenomenon is in fact in its pioneering stages, and that we simply may not know much about its determinants or what changes may be expected in these determinants. On the other hand, if elderly local mobility is indeed less voluntary movement, its more important determinants and their effects may have changed less over time, and have been more validly captured in the studies to date.

IMPLICATIONS

The findings of the present study are relevant to some of the issues raised here. Many of the limitations of the type of studies that comprise the greatest part of the existing literature in the areas of elderly migration and local mobility have been discussed above. The question of the generalizability of the results from such cross-sectional descriptive studies is directly addressed by the present findings. Also, the utility of continuing the recent proliferation of such studies, utilizing the same kinds of possible determinants, for the development of a stronger base from which to begin to develop much needed theory in these areas has been called into question here. The question that begs to be answered involves the types of alternative approaches that might be more constructively employed in for this task. The present findings suggest at least some partial answers.

If our stock of knowledge regarding elderly migration/ mobility is to be meaningfully expanded, it must be through the initiation of studies that examine more than age effects within a single period. Longitudinal research is needed that can show the changes in the effects of variables thought to be associated with elderly migration/ mobility. Perhaps most importantly, this study has demonstrated that the cohort perspective is a methodological approach that can greatly enhance our understanding of observed period effects of possible determinants of elderly mobility. In order to answer the question of whether observed patterns of change in the effects of social/demographic variables on elderly mobility will continue or reverse, we must understand the changes in the social structure that underlie these patterns. Similarly, the question to be answered with respect to the observed age effect on elderly mobility is: Why does it exist? There has been some insightful speculation regarding this question that can be found among the conclusions of descriptive studies in the elderly mobility literature. If the relative economic status of the elderly, for example, is one critical factor, then this should be empirically established.

Although some specific substantive findings result from these analyses, e.g. those regarding the effects of educational attainment, not having a spouse, or the number of children ever born on elderly local mobility, the more important implication of these findings involves the general research and interpretive strategies to which they point. That is, how do these findings point to somewhat more sophisticated methodological approaches than those traditionally employed, and how can they be used to identify directions for the development of a more integrated theoretical framework for elderly migration/mobility? Once we begin to identify sets of factors that differentially affect elderly mobility depending on cohort membership, we can begin to make more general theoretical statements about what has happened in society to bring about the changes that effect cohort differences. For example, in terms of the above-mentioned findings regarding widowhood and number of children ever born, a number of considerations would bear investigation. In recent decades enormous changes in the lifestyles of women have occurred as a result of changes in longevity and differential mortality for males and females. There have also been important changes in family structure and living arrangements, referred to in the development of the hypotheses, that could well underlie changes in the effect of the number of children ever born on elderly local mobility.

It is pointed out above that the micro models tested were generally quite supportive of the hypotheses, and, with regard to interstate migration, much more so than the findings of the aggregate analyses. This indicates that the development of micro models is certainly worth pursuing in future research. Furthermore, the disappointing performance of the micro-level models in terms of explaining variation in the independent variables has important implications for future research. It has often been asserted that micro-level data very seldom yield high R^2s, especially when the phenomenon of interest is a relatively rare event. However, recent articles on the state of theory development in aging research have at least indirectly addressed this issue.

Hernes (1976) and George (1982), in examining structural change in social processes and the convergence of multiple theoretical models in the social psychology of adult development, emphasize the interaction of multiple variables at both the macro- and micro-levels. Maddox and Campbell (1985) assert that research addressing the observed differences in cohorts without considering both micro- and macro-level factors will be seriously flawed. George Maddox (1979) posits that social scientists will for some time be concerned with "partial theoretical perspectives", e.g. life course analysis, rather than with comprehensive grand theory. He further states that life course analysis focuses on selective dimensions of aging rather than the entire aging process, and is centrally concerned with the interaction of micro- and macro-level variables.

Thus both the present findings and authors in the area of aging theory suggest that future research in elderly migration/mobility should involve models that incorporate both individual and macro level data. The inclusion of characteristics of areas of destination and origin as well as individual characteristics might well result in more effective models for explaining elderly mobility behavior.

It should be remembered that there is tremendous value in truly pioneering studies in an area of investigation that eventually tell us that alternative methodological approaches must be utilized if specific kinds of needed progress are to be made. In order to fill the theoretical vacuum in the areas of elderly migration and local mobility, longitudinal research incorporating a cohort perspective as well as examining age, multiple period effects, and examining both micro- and macro- level determinants must be undertaken. These types of studies have the potential of contributing to an emerging body of findings that would help to increase the potential for developing a theoretical framework that can contribute to our understanding of factors that operate on migration and local mobility at the elderly ages when the traditional socioeconomic variables are no longer the prime drivers of such behavior.

One of the major issues raised in this dissertation has been the lack of theoretical development in the area of elderly migration/mobility. The main contribution of the present research in this sense is that it illustrates the difficulty of developing a theory of elderly migration/mobility, by first pointing out and then empirically examining some important dimensions of this phenomenon. This can initially be seen in the maze of relationships set forth in the hypotheses which consider the expected effect of the independent variables on different types of mobility within periods and the effect of cohort membership. These hypotheses can be summarized as follows:

Independent Variable	Interstate Migration		Local Mobility	
	Period	Cohort	Period	Cohort
Female	+	weaker	+	stronger
White	+	weaker	+	weaker
W/O Spouse	-	stronger	+	stronger
Education	+	stronger	-	weaker
Children	-	stronger	+	stronger

The overriding characteristic of these hypothesized relationships is that they do not appear to hang together in any unified manner. That is, in almost all instances, the direction of the expected relationship and/or the effect of cohort membership is inconsistent. Furthermore, the results of the tests of these hypotheses indicate not only period and cohort effects per se, but also differential effects of the independent variables depending on period, cohort membership, or type of mobility, and differences in the results of micro- and macro- level analyses.

The importance of all of these dimensions demonstrates the enormous complexity of understanding elderly migration behavior which has been largely overlooked. The descriptive studies that do exist have given important insights into the differential nature of long- distance versus local elderly mobility, which are recognized and utilized in the present study. However, the present results also show that it is important that we understand how other factors such as period and cohort membership interact to affect changes in the effects of determinants of mobility behavior.

In the case of cohort membership we need to expand and elaborate on the work already done which helps us to understand the changes that have occurred in society that have had a significant impact on the propensity of the elderly to migrate. For example, changes in the sources of income of the elderly have been cited as contributing significantly to the steady increases in levels of elderly migration in recent history. Not only have various government and private programs improved the economic lot of retirees, but these sources of income have also become disassociated with the recipients' place of residence. This has contributed significantly to the ability of the elderly to migrate.

There are other social changes that have affected the relationship of birth cohort and elderly mobility behavior, some of which are included in this study. For example, changes in the relationships and living arrangements of children and parents have had an effect on all types of elderly mobility. Dramatic changes in the roles and lifestyles of women are very important in this respect. Not only has female labor force participation increased, but women are also attaining higher levels of education and increasingly engaging in full-time occupations of higher status than previously.

Changes in marital status and fertility behavior, some related to occupational changes, and others related to changes in longevity and differential male/female mortality have certainly influenced observed historical changes in elderly migration/mobility. In addition to these and other factors that can affect the behavior of cohort members throughout their lives, there are the factors that underlie the observed period effects on elderly migration/mobility. The most often cited period variable used in migration research is some sort of measure of current economic conditions for the period. The effectiveness of period economic indicators in explaining variations in elderly migration/mobility should be further examined. Another example of a factor that might well effect certain types of elderly mobility during given periods involves patterns of urbanization affecting the location or relocation of types of services especially desired or needed by the elderly, trends in neighborhood revitalization that result in the displacement of older residents by the non-elderly, or decline in area conditions that make them unsafe or otherwise undesirable for elderly residents. Another period factor which has had an important impact on increases in elderly migration/mobility behavior is the development of communities designed specifically for elderly residents. The extensive promotion of these communities by their builders, which emphasize all sorts of environmental and other amenities that are important to the elderly, including the company of other older people, has very likely had a significant impact on elderly migration/ mobility.

Future research that seeks to contribute to the development of elderly migration/mobility theory must consider the implications of the above assertions regarding the complexity of this behavior. First, the empirical examination of determinants of cohort and period effects should be undertaken in longitudinal studies. It is necessary to more fully understand the kinds of societal changes and period conditions that have most affected elderly migration/mobility in the past if we are to be able to make more general statements regarding these phenomena. Most significantly, it is of paramount importance that future research in these areas emphasize the interaction of all of the above dimensions or perspectives, because it is the lack of appreciation of the complexity of this behavior that has led to the current impasse in the state of theoretical development in this area.

References

Ables, Ronald P. 1981. Symposium on "Health Behavior, and Aging: Recent Needs." Toronto, Canada: Gerontology Society of America.

Baltes, Paul B. 1968. "Longitudinal and cross-sectional sequences in the study of age and generation effects." *Human Development* 11(3):145-171.

Baltes, Paul B. and John R. Nesselroade. 1970. "Multivariate longitudinal and cross-sectional sequences for analyzing ontogenetic and generational change: a methodological note." *Developmental Psychology* 2(Sept.):163-168.

Baltes, Paul B., H. Reese, and L. Lipsitt. 1980. "Lifespan developmental psychology." *Annual Review of Psychology* 31:65-110.

Baltes, Paul B. and S. L. Willis. 1979. "Life-span developmental psychology, cognitive functioning and social policy." Pp.15-46 in Matilda White Riley (ed.), *Aging From Birth To Death.* Boulder Colo.: Westview Press.

Bengston, V. L. 1981. "Research across the generation gap." In J. Rosenfeld (ed.) *Relationships: The Marriage and Family Reader.* Chicago: Scott, Foresman.

Biggar, Jean C. 1980. "Who moved among the elderly?." *Research on Aging* 2(1)(Mar):73-91.

1980a. "Reassessing elderly Sunbelt migration." *Research on Aging* 2(2) (June):177-190.

Biggar, Jean C., Diane C. Cowper, and Dale E. Yeatts. 1984. "National elderly migration patterns and selectivity." *Research on Aging* 6(2) (June):163- 188.

Biggar, Jean C., Charles F. Longino, Jr., and Cynthia B. Flynn. 1980. "Elderly interstate migration: the impact on sending and receiving states, 1965 to 1970." *Research on Aging* 2(2)(June):217-232.

Bradsher, Julia E., Charles F. Longino, Jr., David J. Jackson, and Rick S. Zimmerman. 1992. "Health and geographic mobility among the recently widowed." *Journal of Gerontology* 47(5): S261-268.

Brim, Orville G., Jr. 1966. "Socialization through the life cycle." In Orville G.Brim, Jr, and Stanton Wheeler (eds.), *Socialization After Childhood: Two Essays*. New York: Wiley.

Bowles, Gladys K. 1980. "Age migration in the United States: a brief review." *Research on Aging* 2(2) (June):137- 140.

Cain, Leonard D. 1964. "Life course and social structure". Pp. 272-309 in Robert E. L. Faris (ed.), *Handbook of Modern Sociology*. Chicago: Rand Mcnally.

Chevan, L. and L. R. Fischer. 1979. "Retirement and interstate migration." *Social Forces* 47:1365-1380.

Clausen, John A. 1968. *Socialization and Society.* Boston: Little Brown.

Cowper, Diane C., and Elizabeth H. Corcoran. 1989. "Older veterans-possible forerunners of migration: migration patterns of the elderly veteran population versus the general elderly population, 1960-1980." *Journal of Applied Gerontology* 8(4):451-464.

Crittenden, John. 1962. "Aging and party affiliation." *Public Opinion Quarterly* 26(Winter):648-657.

Cutler, Neal E. 1969. "Generation, maturation, and party affiliation: a cohort analysis." *Public Opinion Quarterly* 33(Winter):583-591.

Duncan, Otis Dudley. 1959. "Human ecology and population studies." Pp. 716 in Philip M. Hauser and Otis Dudley Duncan (eds.), *The Study of Population, an Inventory and Appraisal.* Chicago: The University of Chicago Press.

Eisenstadt, S. N. 1956. *From Generation to Generation: Age Groups and Social Structure.* Glencoe, Ill.: Free Press.

Elder, Glen H., Jr. 1979. "Historical change in life patterns and personality." Pp. 118-159 in Paul B. Baltes and Orville G. Brim, Jr. (eds.), *Life-Span Development and Behavior, Vol. II.* New York: Academic Press.

Eldrige, Hope T. 1964. "A cohort approach to the analysis of migration differentials." *Demography* 1:212-219.

Folger, John K. 1958. "Models in migration." Pp.160-161 in *Selected Studies of Migration Since World War II.* New York: Milbank Memorial Fund.

Flynn, Cynthia B. 1980. "General versus aged interstate migration, 1965-1970." *Research on Aging* 2 (2):165-176.

France. 1964. *General census of population, 1962; results from the five-percent sample; Population, households, dwellings, other living quarters; Summary for France as a whole.*

Frey, William H. 1986. "Lifecourse migration and redistribution of the elderly across U.S. regions and metropolitan areas." *Economic Outlook* USA 13(2): 10-15.

Fuguitt, Glenn V. and Stephen J. Tordella. 1980. "Elderly net migration: the new trend of nonmetropolitan population change." *Research on Aging* 2(2) (June):191-204.

Glenn, Norval D. 1980. "Values, attitudes, and beliefs." Pp. 596-640 in Orville G. Brim, Jr. and J. Kagan (eds.), *Constancy and Change in Human Development.* Cambridge, Mass.:Harvard University Press.

Glenn, Norval D. and Ted Hefner. 1972. "Further evidence on aging and party identification." *Public Opinion Quarterly* 36 (Spring):31-74.

Golant, Steven M. 1987. "Residential moves by elderly persons to U.S. Central Cities, suburbs, and rural areas." *Journal of Gerontology* 42(5):534-539.

1980. "Future directions for elderly migration research." *Research on Aging* 2(2) (June):271-280.

Goldscheider, Calvin. 1966. "Differential residential mobility and the older population." *Journal of Gerontology* 21:103-108.

Hastings, D. V. and L. G. Berry (eds.) 1979. *Cohort Analysis: A Collection of Interdisciplinary Readings.* Oxford, OH: Scripps Foundation For Research in Population Problems.

Heaton, Tim B., William B. Clifford, and Glenn V. Fuguitt. 1980. "Changing patterns of retirement migration: movement between metropolitan and nonmetropolitan areas." *Research on Aging* 2(1) (March):93-104.

Hobcraft, John, Jane Menken, and Samuel Preston. 1982. "Age, period, and cohort effects in demography: A review. *Population Index* 48:4-43.

Hogan, D. P. 1981. *Transitions and Social Change.* New York: Academic Press.

Hogan, D. P. and M. Pazul. 1981. "The career strategies of black men." *Social Forces* 59:1217-1228.

Jackson, David J., Charles F. Longino, Rick S. Zimmerman, and Julia E. Bradsher. 1991. "Environmental adjustments to declining functional ability: residential mobility and living arrangements." *Research on Aging* 13(3): 289-309.

Japan, Bureau of Statistics. 1962. *1960 Population Census of Japan, Vol. 2, One Percent Sample Tabulation, Part 2, Migration.*

Keyfitz, Nathan. 1972. "Oscillations in a demographic-economic Model." Madison, Wisconsin: Unpublished paper presented at the Conference on Population Dynamics, sponsored by the Mathematics Research Center, University of Wisconsin, July, 1972.

Klecka, William R. 1971. "Applying political generations to the study of political behavior: a cohort analysis." *Public Opinion Quarterly* 35 (Fall):358-373.

Lansing, J. B. and E. Mueller. 1967. *The Geographic Mobility of Labor*. Ann Arbor, MI: Survey Research Center.

Lazarsfield, Paul F., Bernard Berelson, and Hazel Gaudet. [1944] 1960. *The People's Choice*. New York: Columbia University Press.

Lee, Everett S. 1980. "Migration of the aged." *Research on Aging* 2(2):131-136.

1966. "A theory of Migration." *Demography* 3:47-57.

Lawton, M. P., M. H. Klwban, and D. A. Carlson. 1973. "The inner city resident: to move or not to move." *Gerontologist* 13:443-448.

Lenzer, A. 1965. "Mobility patterns among the aged." *Gerontologist* 5:12-15.

Linton, Ralph. 1942. "Age and sex categories." *American Sociological Review* 7:589-603.

Longino, Charles F., Jr. 1980. "Residential relocation of older people: metropolitan and nonmetropolitan." *Research on Aging* 2(2):205-216.

1979. "Going home: aged return migration in the United States 1965-1970." *Journal of Gerontology* 34(5):736-745.

Longino, Charles F., David J. Jackson, Rick S. Zimmerman, and Julia E. Bradsher. 1991. "The second move: health and geographic mobility." *Journal of Gerontology* 46(4):S218- 224.

Longino, Charles F., Victor W. Marshall, Larry C. Mullins, and Richard D. Tucker. 1991. "On the nesting of snowbirds: a question about seasonal and permanent migrants." *Journal of Applied Gerontology* 10(2):157-168

Longino, Charles F., and William J. Serow. 1992. "Regional differences in the characteristics of elderly return migrants." *Journal of Gerontology* 47(1):S38-43.

Mannheim, K. [1928] 1952. "The Problem of Generations." In Kecskmenti (ed.), *Essays on the Sociology of Knowledge.* London:Routledge and Kegan Paul.

Mason, Karen Oppenheim, William M. Mason, H. H. Winsborough, and W. Kenneth Poole. 1972. "Some methodological issues in cohort analysis of archival data." *American Sociological Review* 38 (April):242-258.

Michael, Robert T., Victor R. Fuchs, and Sharon Scott. 1980. "Changes in the propensity to live alone: 1950-1976." *Demography* 17:39-56.

Mitchell, Jean M. and J. S. Butler. 1986. "Arthritis and the earnings of men: an analysis incorporating selection bias." *Journal of Health Economics* 5(7) (March):81-98.

Olsen, Randall J. 1980. "A least squares correction for selectivity bias." *Econometrica* 48(7) (Nov.): 1815-1820.

Oppenheim, Karen. 1970. *Voting in recent American presidential elections.* Chicago: University of Chicago, unpublished Ph.D. dissertation.

Parsons, Talcott. 1942. "Age and sex in the social structure of the United States." In Talcott Parsons, *Essays in Sociological Theory, Pure and Applied.* Glencoe, Ill.: Free Press.

Pastalan, L. A. 1975. "Research in environment and aging: an alternative to theory." In P. G. Windley et al. (eds.), *Theory Development in Environment and Aging.* Washington, D.C.: National Institute on Aging.

Pitcher, Brian L., William F. Stinner, and Michael B. Toney. 1985. "Patterns of migration propensity for black and white American men." *Research on Aging* 7 (March):94-120.

Riley, Matilda White. 1978. "Aging, social change, and the power of ideas." *Daedalus* 107:39-52.

          1973. "Aging and cohort succession: interpretations and misinterpretations." *Public Opinion Quarterly* 37:35-49.

Riley, Matilda White, M. Johnson, and A. Foner. 1972. *Aging and Society, Vol. III, A Sociology of Age Stratification.* New York: Russell Sage Foundation.

Rives, Norfleet W., Jr., and William J. Serow. 1981. "Interstate migration of the elderly." *Research on Aging* 3(3)(Sept): 259-278.

Rodgers, Willard L. 1982. "Estimable functions of age, period, and cohort effects." *American Sociological Review* 47 (December):774-787.

Rogers, Andrei, and John Watkins. 1987. "General versus elderly interstate migration and population redistribution in the United States." *Research on Aging* 9(4):483-529.

Ryder, Norman B. 1965. "The cohort as a concept in the study of social change." *American Sociological Review* 30:843-861.

1964. "Notes on the concept of a population." *American Journal of Sociology* 69:447-463.

Serow, William J. 1988. "Why the elderly move: cross-national comparisons." *Research on Aging* 9(4):582-597.

1987. "Determinants of interstate migration: differences between elderly and nonelderly movers." *Journal of Gerontology* 42(1):95-100.

Serow, William J., and Douglas A. Charity. 1988. "Return migration of the elderly in the United States: recent trends." *Research on Aging* 10(2):155-168.

Shaw, R. P. 1975. *Migration Theory and Fact*. Philadelphia: Regional Science Research Institute.

Shryock, Henry S., Jr. 1964. *Population Mobility Within the United States*. Chicago: Community and Family Study Center, University of Chicago.

Sorokin, Pitrim A. 1947. *Society, Culture and Personality*. New York: Harper and Brothers.

1941. *Social and Cultural Dynamics: Basic Problems, Principles, and Methods, Vol. 4*. New York: American Book Company.

Speare, Alden, Jr. 1974. "Residential satisfaction as an intervening variable in residential mobility. *Demography* 11:173-188.

Spear, Alden, Jr., Roger Avery, and Leora Lawton. 1991. "Disability, residential mobility, and changes in living arrangements." *Journal of Gerontology* 46(3):S133-142.

Spear, Alden, Jr., and Judith W. Meyer. 1988. "Types of elderly residential mobility and their determinants." *Journal of Gerontology* 43(3):S74-81.

Starr, Bernice C. 1972. "The Community." Pp.198-235 in Matilda White Riley, Marilyn Johnson, and Anne Foner (eds.), *Aging and Society: A Sociology of Age Stratification, Vol. III.* New York: Russell Sage Foundation.

Stinner, William F., Brian L. Pitcher, and Michael B. Toney. 1985. "Discriminators of migration propensity among black and white men in the middle and later years." *Research on Aging* 7(4) December:535-562.

Taeuber, Karl E. 1966. "Cohort Migration." *Demography* 3:416- 423.

Thomas, Dorothy Swaine. 1938. *Research Memorandum on Migration Differentials.* New York: Social Science Research Council.

Torrey, Barbara Boyle. 1982. "The lengthening of retirement." Pp. 181-196 in Matilda White Riley, Ronald P. Abeles, and Michael S. Teitelbaum (eds.), *AAAS Selected Symposium 79, Aging from Birth to Death: Sociotemporal Perspectives, Vol. II.* Boulder Colo.: Westview Press.

Uhlenberg, Peter. 1979. "Demographic change and problems of the aged. Pp. 153-166 in Matilda White Riley (ed.), *Aging from Birth to Death: Interdisciplinary Perspectives, Vol. 1*. Boulder, Colo.: Westview Press.

Voss, Paul R., Ronald J Gunderson, and Robert Manchin. 1988. "Death taxes and elderly interstate migration." *Research on Aging* 10(3):420-450.

Winsborough, H. H. 1979. "Changes in the transition to adulthood." In Matilda White Riley (ed.), *Aging from Birth to Death: Interdisciplinary Perspectives*. Boulder, Col.:Westview Press.

1978. "Statistical histories of the life cycle of birth cohorts: The transition from schoolboy to adult male."Pp. 231-259 in K. E. Taeuber et al (eds.), *Social Demography*. New York: Academic Press.

1972. "Age, period, cohort and education effects on earnings by race-an experiment with a sequence of cross-sectional surveys." Madison, Wisconsin: University of Wisconsin, Center for Demography and Ecology, unpublished paper presented at the July, 1972 Russell Sage Foundation Conference on Social Indicator Models.

Wiseman, Robert F. 1980. "Why older people move: theoretical issues." *Research on Aging* 2(2)(June):141-154.

Yeatts, Dale E., Jeanne C. Biggar, and Charles F. Longino, Jr. 1987. "Distance versus destination: stream selectivity of elderly interstate migrants." *Journal of Gerontology* 42(3):288-294.

INDEX